SQL Server Interview Questions and Answers (Updated 2021)

Pinal Dave

SQL Server Performance Tuning Expert

Vinod Kumar

SQL Server Performance Tuning Expert

Pinal Dave

Pinal Dave is an SQL Server Performance Tuning Expert and independent consultant with over 17 years of hands-on experience. He holds a Masters of Science degree and numerous database certifications.

Pinal has authored 12 SQL Server database books and 37 Pluralsight courses. To freely share his knowledge and help others build their expertise, Pinal has also written more than 5,500 database tech articles on his blog at https://blog.sqlauthority.com.

Pinal is an experienced and dedicated professional with a deep commitment to flawless customer service. If you need help with any SQL Server Performance Tuning Issues, please feel free to reach out at pinal@sqlauthority.com. You can find Pinal at the following coordinates:

Blog: https://blog.sqlauthority.com

Twitter: https://twitter.com/pinaldave

LinkedIn: http://www.linkedin.com/in/pinaldave

Facebook: http://facebook.com/SQLAuth

YouTube: https://www.youtube.com/pinaldavesqlauthority

For free SQL Server Performance Tuning Tips and Tricks subscribe here: https://go.sqlauthority.com

---

Vinod Kumar

Vinod Kumar currently works as Director for Cloud Solutions Architect working with Asia Global Downstream Customers at Microsoft. He has more than 2 decades of experience working on various roles spanning product development, evangelism, technical architecture, people leadership, Research & Development and more. He holds 30+ Microsoft Certification on various technologies till date and counting. Before joining Microsoft, he was Microsoft MVP – SQL Server for more than 3 years.

Acknowledgement

I must express my deepest gratitude to my friend Rick Morelan, who had co-authored many books with us and mentored us to become better author and human. Vinod had the unique capability to bring the best from the people and always there whenever I need support and guidance.

Today we are using computers for various activities, motor vehicle for travelling to places and mobile phones for conversation. How many of us, can claim the invention of the microprocessor, the basic wheel or the telegraph? Well, the same way this book was not written overnight. The journey of this book-writing goes many years back and many individuals to thank for.

To begin with, we want to thank all those interviewers who reject interviewees by saying they need to know the key things' besides having high grades in class. The whole concept of interview questions and answer revolves around knowing 'the key things'.

The core concept of this book will be always evolving and I am sure many of you will come along with us and give your suggestions to make this book always a key reference for anybody who wants to start with SQL Server. Today we want to acknowledge the fact that you will keep the core concept of this book at heart and help us to keep this book always alive and with the latest information. We want to thank you for the same.

About this book

As representatives from the IT community, all of us have had our own experiences of attending interviews – clearing or close to clearing and sometimes with tons of questions and doubts failing miserably. These stories are in the most pleasant or not so pleasant memories of our mind and we will assure you this book will kindle those memories for sure. We have taken tons of interviews and most of the interviews are not revolving around how deep technical and internals you know about the subject – but it revolves around how good you are with the basics.

To clear an interview, one doesn't need to know inside-out of a subject, and subjects like "SQL Server" so vast that every single day we learn something new with this product, and even a complete lifetime will fly off if we keep doing this. Again, the various roles one can get into for products like SQL Server are from Database Developer, Database Modelers, Database Architect, Database Administrator and many more. Hence, this book is geared towards demystifying and a refresher for memories on the fundamentals which sometimes are the most important things to clear any type of interview for any role. Some of the concepts discussed are generic and are not tied to any specific version of SQL Server, but most of it the new features introduced with SQL Server have been included in this book.

This book is not a shortcut or a sure to crack interview guide but this book gets you prepared in an organized manner. Let us also assure you this is neither a completely comprehensive guide but surely is a great starter nevertheless. Use this to guide you and be mentally prepared for the big day. When faced with this big day, we get overwhelmed and confused about where to start our preparation. And this book is just that secret recipe in your arsenal to get geared up. Sometimes these basics will help you narrow to a solution quickly when given a scenario.

Now this book's flow is "Question & Answer" mode from start till the end to help you grasp the concepts faster and to the point. Once you get an understanding of concepts, then if we are twisted with the concept in a scenario it becomes easy to solve them. Most companies have a typical way to do interviews which are based on the scenario as per their environment and these are just combinations of the concepts to fit their need and SLA.

Though each of these chapters is bucketed for convenience we highly recommend reading each of the sections nevertheless irrespective of the roles you might be doing as each of the sections have some interesting trivia's working with SQL Server. In the industry, the role of accidental DBA's especially with SQL Server is so common. Hence if you have performed the role of DBA for a short stink and want to brush-up your fundamentals then the respective sections will be a great skim.

Final Note:

After you complete reading this book, do not stop your learning. There are over 301 SQL Server Interview Questions and Answers available for free reading at here: https://blog.sqlauthority.com/category/sql-interview-questions-and-answers/

TABLE OF CONTENT

Consulting

Is your SQL Server running slow and you want to speed it up without sharing server credentials? In my **Comprehensive Database Performance Health Check**, we can work together remotely and resolve your biggest performance troublemakers in **less than 4 hours**.

Once you learn my business secrets, you will fix the majority of problems in the future.

Training

Have you ever opened any PowerPoint deck when you face SQL Server Performance Tuning emergencies? **SQL Server Performance Tuning Practical Workshop** is my MOST popular training with no PowerPoint presentations and **100% practical demonstrations**.

Essentially I share my business secrets to optimize SQL Server performance.

For **SQL Server Emergency Help**, you can reach out to me at *pinal@sqlauthority.com* with words ***URGENT*** in the email subject line for other services mention "*Comprehensive Database Performance Health Check*".

Section 1: Database Concepts with SQL SERVER

What is RDBMS?

Relational Database Management Systems (RDBMS) are database management systems that maintain data records and indices in tables. Relationships may be created and maintained across and among the data and tables. In a relational database, relationships between data items are expressed using tables. Interdependencies among these tables are expressed by data values rather than by pointers. This allows for a high degree of data independence. An RDBMS can recombine the data items from different files, providing powerful tools for data usage.

What are the Properties of the Relational Tables?

Relational tables have the following six properties:

- Values are atomic.
- Column values are of the same kind.
- The sequence of columns is insignificant.
- The sequence of rows is insignificant.
- Each column must have a unique name.

What is Normalization?

Database normalization is a data design and organization process applied to data structures based on rules that help to build relational databases. In relational database design, the process of organizing data to minimize redundancy is called normalization. Normalization usually involves dividing database data into different tables and defining relationships between the tables. The objective is to isolate data so that additions, deletions, and modifications of a field can be made in just one table and then retrieved through the rest of the database via the defined relationships.

What is De-normalization?

De-normalization is the process of attempting to optimize the performance of a database by adding redundant data. It is sometimes necessary because current DBMSs implement the relational model poorly. A true relational DBMS would allow for a fully normalized database at the logical level while providing physical storage of data that is tuned for high performance. De-normalization is a technique to move from higher to lower normal forms of database modeling to speed up database access.

How is ACID property related to Database?

ACID (an acronym for Atomicity Consistency Isolation Durability) is a concept that Database Professionals generally look for while evaluating relational databases and application architectures. For a reliable database, all these four attributes should be achieved:

Atomicity is an all-or-none rule for Database modifications.

Consistency guarantees that a transaction never leaves your database in a half-finished state.

Isolation keeps transactions separated from each other until they are finished.

Durability guarantees that the database will keep track of pending changes in such a way that the server can recover from an abnormal termination and committed transactions will not be lost.

What are the different Normalization Forms?

There are many different types of normalization. Let us see the list.

1NF: Eliminate Repeating Groups

Make a separate table for each set of related attributes, and give each table a primary key. Each field contains at most one value from its attribute domain.

2NF: Eliminate Redundant Data

If an attribute depends on only part of a multi-valued key, then remove it to a separate table.

3NF: Eliminate Columns Not Dependent On Key

If attributes do not contribute to a description of the key, then remove them from a separate table. All attributes must be directly dependent on the primary key.

BCNF: Boyce-Codd Normal Form

If there are non-trivial dependencies between candidate key attributes, then separate them into distinct tables.

4NF: Isolate Independent Multiple Relationships

No table may contain two or more 1:n or n:m relationships that are not directly related.

5NF: Isolate Semantically Related Multiple Relationships

There may be practical constrains on information that justifies separating logically related many-to-many relationships.

ONF: Optimal Normal Form

A model limited to only simple (elemental) facts, as expressed in Object Role Model notation.

DKNF: Domain-Key Normal Form

A model-free from all modification anomalies is said to be in DKNF.

Remember, these normalization guidelines are cumulative. For a database to be in 3NF, it must first fulfil all the criteria of a 2NF and 1NF database.

What is a Stored Procedure?

A stored procedure (SP) is a named group of SQL statements that have been previously created and stored in the server database. Stored procedures accept input parameters so that a single procedure can be used over the network by several clients using different input data. And when the procedure is modified, all clients automatically get the new version. Stored procedures reduce network traffic and improve performance. Stored procedures can be used to help ensure the integrity of the database logic. Typical System Stored Procedures are - sp_helpdb, sp_renamedb, sp_depends etc.

What is a Trigger?

A trigger is a SQL procedure or SQLCLR Code that initiates an action when an event (INSERT, DELETE or UPDATE) occurs. Triggers are stored in and managed by the DBMS. Triggers can be used to maintain the referential integrity of data by systematically changing the data. A trigger cannot be called or executed; DBMS automatically fires the trigger as a result of a data modification to the associated table. Triggers can be considered to be similar to stored procedures in that both consist of procedural logic that is stored at the database level. Stored procedures, however, are not event-driven and are not attached to a specific table as triggers are. Stored procedures are explicitly executed by invoking a CALL to the procedure while triggers are implicitly executed. Besides, triggers can also execute stored procedures.

Nested Trigger: A trigger can also contain INSERT, UPDATE and DELETE logic within itself; so when the trigger is fired because of data modification, it can also cause another data modification, thereby firing another trigger. A trigger that contains data modification logic within itself is called a nested trigger.

What are the Different Types of Triggers?

There are three types of Triggers.

DML Trigger

There are two types of DML Triggers

a. Instead of Trigger
   Instead of Triggers are fired in place of the triggering action such as an insert, update, or delete.
b. After Trigger
   After triggers execute following the triggering action, such as an insert, update, or delete.

DDL Trigger

This type of trigger is fired against Drop Table, Create Table, Alter Table. DDL Triggers are always After Triggers.

Logon Trigger

This type of trigger is fired against a LOGON event before a user session is established to the SQL Server.

What is a View?

A view can be thought of as a stored query accessible as a virtual table. It can be used for retrieving data as well as updating or deleting rows. Rows updated or deleted in the view are updated or deleted in the table the view was created with. It should also be noted that as data in the original table changes, so does the data in the view as views are the way to look at parts of the original table. The results of using a view are not permanently stored in the database. The data accessed through a view is constructed using standard T-SQL select command and can come from one-to-many different base tables or even other views.

What is an Index?

An index is a physical structure containing pointers to the data. Indices are created in an existing table to locate rows more quickly and efficiently. It is possible to create an index on one or more columns of a table, and each index is given a name. The users cannot see the indexes; they are just used to speed up queries. Effective indexes are one of the best ways to improve performance in a database application. A table scan happens when there is no index available to help a query. In a table scan, the SQL Server examines every row in the table to satisfy the query results. Table scans are sometimes unavoidable, but on large tables, scans have a terrific impact on performance.

What is an Indexed View?

A view that has a unique clustered index is referred to as an indexed view. The biggest feature of Indexed views are -

- The view's result set is materialized immediately and persisted in physical storage in the database
- It also saves the overhead of performing any costly operation (like Joins, Aggregates etc) during execution time

The query can reference the indexed view directly or the query optimizer can select the view if it determines that the view can be substituted for some or all of the query in the lowest-cost query plan.

Why can't I use Outer Join in an Indexed View?

Rows can logically disappear from an indexed view based on OUTER JOIN when you insert data into a base table. This makes incrementally updating OUTER JOIN views relatively complex to implement, and the performance of the implementation would be slower than for views based on standard (INNER) JOIN.

What is a Linked Server?

A linked server configuration enables SQL Server to execute commands against OLE DB data sources on remote servers. With a linked server, you can create very clean, easy-to-follow SQL statements that allow remote data to be retrieved, joined and combined with local data. The ability to issue distributed queries and perform commands with transactions on heterogeneous sources are one of the keys to using Linked Servers.
Stored Procedures sp_addlinkedserver, sp_addlinkedsrvlogin will be used to add a new Linked Server and sp_linkedservers is used to list all the Linked Servers defined on the Server.

What is a Cursor?

A cursor is a database object used by applications in the procedural logic to manipulate data on a row-by-row basis, instead of the typical SQL commands that operate on all / parts of rows as a set of data.

To work with a cursor, we need to perform some steps in the following order:

- Declare cursor
- Open cursor
- Fetch row from the cursor
- Process fetched row
- Close cursor
- Deallocate cursor

What is subquery? Explain the Properties of a Subquery?

Subqueries are often referred to as sub-selects as they allow a SELECT statement to be executed within the body of another SQL statement. A subquery is executed by enclosing it in a set of parentheses. Subqueries are generally used to return rows as an atomic value although they may be used to compare values against multiple rows with the IN keyword.

Some properties of typical Subqueries:

- A subquery is a SELECT statement that is nested within another T-SQL statement.
- A subquery SELECT statement if executed independently of the T-SQL statement, in which it is nested, will return a resultset. This implies that a subquery SELECT statement can stand alone, and it does not depend on the statement in which it is nested.
- A subquery SELECT statement can return any number of values and can be found in the column list of a SELECT statement, and FROM, GROUP BY, HAVING, and/or ORDER BY clauses of a T-SQL statement.
- A subquery can also be used as a parameter to a function call. A subquery can be used anywhere an expression can be used.

What are Different Types of Join?

Inner Join

A join that displays only the rows that have a match in both joined tables is known as inner Join. This is the default type of join in the Query and View Designer.

Outer Join

A join that includes rows even if they do not have related rows in the joined table is an Outer Join. You can create three different variations of outer join to specify the unmatched rows to be included:

- Left Outer Join: In Left Outer Join, all the rows in the first-named table, i.e. "left" table, which appears leftmost in the JOIN clause, are included. Unmatched rows in the right table do not appear.

- Right Outer Join: In Right Outer Join, all the rows in the second-named table, i.e. "right" table, which appears rightmost in the JOIN clause are included. Unmatched rows in the left table are not included.

- Full Outer Join: In Full Outer Join, all the rows in all joined tables are included, whether they are matched or not.

Cross Join

A cross join that does not have a WHERE clause produces the Cartesian product of the tables involved in the join. The size of a Cartesian product result set is *the number of rows in the first table multiplied by the number of rows in the second table*. A common example is when a company wants to combine each product with a pricing table to analyse each product at each price.

Self-Join

This is a special case when one table joins itself with one or two aliases to avoid confusion. A self-join can be of any type, as long as the joined tables are the same. A self-join is rather unique in that it involves a relationship with only one table. A common example is when a company has a hierarchal reporting structure whereby one member of staff reports to another or a typical part with subparts hierarchy. Self-Join can be Outer Join or Inner Join.

Define User-defined Functions and their different variations?

User-defined Functions allow defining its T-SQL functions that can accept zero or more parameters and return a single scalar data value or a table data type.

Different Types of User-Defined Functions created are as follows:

Scalar User-defined Function

A scalar user-defined function returns one of the scalar data types. Text, ntext, image, timestamp, Error Handling, XML data types are not supported. These are the type of user-defined functions that most developers are used to in other programming languages too.

Inline Table-Value User-defined Function

An inline table-valued user-defined function returns a table data type and is an exceptional alternative to a view as the user-defined function can pass parameters into a T-SQL select command and in essence provide us with a parameterized, non-updateable view of the underlying tables.

Multi-Statement Table-Value User-defined Function

A multi-statement table-valued user-defined function returns a table, and it is also an exceptional alternative to a view as the function can support multiple T-SQL statements to build the final result where the view is limited to a single SELECT statement. Also, the ability to pass parameters into a T-SQL select command or a group of them gives us the capability to in essence create a parameterized, non-updateable view of the data in the underlying tables. Within the create function command, you must define the table structure that is being returned. After creating this type of user-defined function, It can be used in the FROM clause of a T-SQL command unlike the behaviour encountered while using a stored procedure which can also return record sets.

What is the Difference between a User Defined Function and a Stored Procedure?

UDF can be used in the SQL statements anywhere in the WHERE/HAVING/SELECT section, whereas Stored procedures cannot be. UDFs that return tables can be treated as another rowset. This can be used in JOINs with other tables. Inline UDF's can be thought of as views that take parameters and can be used in JOINs and other Rowset operations.

What is Identity?

Identity (or AutoNumber) is a column that automatically generates numeric values. There can be only one IDENTITY Column in a given table inside SQL Server. A start and increment value can be set, but most DBAs leave these at 1. A GUID column also generates numbers; the value of identity cannot be controlled. Identity/GUID columns do not need to be indexed.

What is the Correct Order of the Logical Query Processing Phases?

The correct order of the Logical Query Processing Phases is as follows:

1. FROM
2. ON
3. OUTER
4. WHERE
5. GROUP BY
6. CUBE | ROLLUP
7. HAVING
8. SELECT
9. DISTINCT
10. ORDER BY
11. TOP

What is the PRIMARY KEY?

A PRIMARY KEY constraint is a unique identifier for a row within a database table. Every table should have a primary key constraint to uniquely identify each row, and only one primary key constraint can be created for each table. The primary key constraints are used to enforce entity integrity.

What is the FOREIGN KEY?

A FOREIGN KEY constraint prevents any actions that would destroy links between tables with the corresponding data keys. A foreign key in one table points to a primary key / unique key on another table. Foreign keys prevent actions that would leave rows with foreign key values when there are no primary keys with that value. The foreign key constraints are used to enforce referential integrity.

What is UNIQUE KEY Constraint?

A UNIQUE constraint enforces the uniqueness of the values in a set of columns; so no duplicate values are entered. The unique key constraints are used to enforce entity integrity as the primary key constraints.

What is CHECK Constraint?

A CHECK constraint is used to limit the values that can be placed in a column. The check constraints are used to enforce domain integrity.

What is NOT NULL Constraint?

A NOT NULL constraint enforces that the column will not accept null values. The not null constraints are used to enforce domain integrity, as the check constraints.

What is DEFAULT Definition?

A DEFAULT definition is used to add values into a column when values were omitted. The default value must be compatible with the data type of the column to which the DEFAULT definition applies.

What are Catalog Views?

Catalog views return information that is used by the SQL Server Database Engine. Catalog Views are the most general interface to the catalog metadata and provide the most efficient way to obtain, transform, and present customized forms of this information. All user-available catalog metadata is exposed through catalog views.

Section 2: Generic Questions & Answers for DBAs and Devs

What is OLTP (Online Transaction Processing)?

In OLTP –online transaction processing systems, relational database design uses the discipline of data modeling and generally follows the Codd rules of data normalization to ensure absolute data integrity. Using these rules, complex information is broken down into its most simple structures (a table) where all of the individual atomic level elements relate to each other and satisfy the normalization rules.

What are Pessimistic Lock and Optimistic Lock?

Optimistic Locking is a strategy where you read a record, take note of a version number and check that the version hasn't changed before you write the record back. If the record is dirty (i.e. different version to yours), then you abort the transaction and the user can re-start the transaction with the new data and update appropriately.

Pessimistic Locking is when you lock the record for your exclusive use until you have finished with it. It has much better integrity than optimistic locking but requires you to be careful with your application design to avoid Deadlocks.

What are Different Types of Locks?

- **Shared Locks:** Used for operations that do not change or update data (read-only operations), such as a SELECT statement.
- **Update Locks:** Used on resources that can be updated. It prevents a common form of deadlock that occurs when multiple sessions are reading, locking, and potentially updating resources later.
- **Exclusive Locks:** Used for data-modification operations, such as INSERT, UPDATE, or DELETE. It ensures that multiple updates cannot be made to the same resource at the same time.
- **Intent Locks:** Used to establish a lock hierarchy. The types of intent locks are as follows: intent shared (IS), intent exclusive (IX), and shared with intent exclusive (SIX).
- **Schema Locks:** Used when an operation dependent on the schema of a table is executing. The types of schema locks are schema modification (Sch-M) and schema stability (Sch-S).
- **Bulk Update Locks:** Used when bulk-copying data into a table and the TABLOCK hint is specified.

What is the Difference between Update Lock and Exclusive Lock?

When Exclusive Lock is on any process, no other lock can be placed on that row or table. Every other process has to wait till Exclusive Lock completes its tasks.

Update Lock is a type of Exclusive Lock, except that it can be placed on the row which already has Shared Lock on it. Update Lock reads the data of the row which has the Shared Lock as soon as the Update Lock is ready to change the data it converts itself to the Exclusive Lock.

What is new in lock escalation in SQL Server?

Lock escalation is one of the lesser-known phenomena inside SQL Server. SQL Server uses this to minimize the overhead of locking too many structures by escalating the locks from just rows to a page to tables. Lock Escalation option in alter table allows disabling of lock escalation on the table.

What is NOLOCK Hint?

Using the NOLOCK query optimizer hint is generally considered good practice to improve concurrency on a busy system especially for Reporting workloads. When the NOLOCK hint is included in a SELECT statement, no locks are taken when data is read. The result is a Dirty Read, which means that another process could be updating the data at the exact time you are reading it. There are no guarantees that your query will retrieve the most recent data.

The performance advantage is that your reading of data will not block updates from taking place, and updates will not block your reading of data. SELECT statements generally take Shared (Read) locks which are avoided because of the hints. This means that multiple SELECT statements are allowed simultaneous access, but other processes are blocked from modifying the data.

What is the difference between DELETE and TRUNCATE Commands?

Delete command removes the rows from a table based on the condition that we provide with a WHERE clause. Truncate will remove all the rows from a table, and there will be no data in the table after we run the truncate command.

TRUNCATE

- TRUNCATE is faster and uses fewer system and transaction log resources than DELETE.
- TRUNCATE removes the data by deallocating the data pages used to store the table's data, and only the page deallocations are recorded in the transaction log.
- TRUNCATE removes all the rows from a table, but the table structure, its columns, constraints, indexes and so on remain. The counter used by an identity for new rows is reset to the seed for the column.
- You cannot use TRUNCATE TABLE on a table referenced by a FOREIGN KEY constraint. As TRUNCATE TABLE is not logged, it cannot activate a trigger.
- TRUNCATE cannot be rolled back unless it is used in TRANSACTION.
- TRUNCATE is a DDL Command.
- TRUNCATE resets the identity of the table

DELETE

- DELETE removes rows one at a time and records an entry in the transaction log for each deleted row.
- If you want to retain the identity counter, use DELETE instead. If you want to remove the table definition and its data, use the DROP TABLE statement.
- DELETE can be used with or without a WHERE clause
- DELETE activates Triggers.
- DELETE can be rolled back.
- DELETE is DML Command.
- DELETE does not reset the identity of the table.

What is Connection Pooling and why it is used?

To minimize the cost of opening and closing connections, ADO.NET uses an optimization technique called connection pooling. The pooler maintains ownership of the physical connection. It manages connections by keeping alive a set of active connections for each given connection configuration. Whenever a user calls Open on a connection, the pooler looks for an available connection in the pool. If a pooled connection is available, it returns it to the caller instead of opening a new connection. When the application calls close on the connection, the pooler returns it to the pooled set of active connections instead of closing it. Once the connection is returned to the pool, it is ready to be reused on the next Open call.

What is the difference between UNION and UNION ALL?

UNION

The UNION command is used to select related information from two tables, much like the JOIN command. However, when using the UNION command all selected columns need to be of the same data type. With UNION, only distinct values are selected.

UNION ALL

UNION ALL command is equal to the UNION command, except that UNION ALL selects all values.

The difference between UNION and UNION ALL is that UNION ALL will not eliminate duplicate rows, instead, it just pulls all rows from all the tables fitting your query specifics and combines them into a table.

What is Collation?

Collation refers to a set of rules that determine how data is sorted and compared. Character data is sorted using rules that define the correct character sequence with options for specifying case-sensitivity, accent marks, Kana character types, and character width.

What are Different Types of Collation Sensitivity?

Case sensitivity - A and a, B and b, etc.

Accent sensitivity - a and á, o and ó, etc.

Kana Sensitivity - When Japanese Kana characters Hiragana and Katakana are treated differently, it is called Kana sensitive.

Width sensitivity – When a single-byte character (half-width) and the same character represented as a double-byte character (full-width) are treated differently, it is width sensitive.

How to check Collation and Compatibility level for a database?

The following query can be used to know the same:

```
SELECT compatibility_level, collation_name
FROM sys.databases
WHERE name ='YOUR DATABASE NAME HERE'
```

What is Dirty Read?

A dirty read occurs when two operations, say, read and write occur together giving the incorrect or in-transit data. Suppose, User1 changed a row but did not commit the changes and User2 reads the uncommitted data but his view of the data may be wrong so that is Dirty Read.

What is Snapshot Isolation?

SQL Server 2005 introduces a new snapshot isolation level to enhance concurrency for OLTP applications. Once snapshot isolation is enabled, updated row versions for each transaction are maintained in tempdb. So, for any transaction that requests a record that is in between a transaction, the last consistent committed value is shown to the user.

What is the difference between a HAVING clause and a WHERE clause?

HAVING specifies a search condition for a group by or an aggregate. But the difference is that HAVING can be used only with the SELECT statement. HAVING is typically used with a GROUP BY clause. Having Clause is used only with the GROUP BY function in a query, whereas WHERE Clause is applied to each row before they are part of the GROUP BY function in a query.

What is B-Tree?

The database server uses a B-tree structure to organize index information. B-Tree generally has the following types of index pages or nodes:

- *Root node:* A root node contains node pointers to only one branch node.
- *Branch nodes:* A branch node contains pointers to leaf nodes or other branch nodes, which can be two or more.
- *Leaf nodes:* A leaf node contains index items and horizontal pointers to other leaf nodes, which can be many.

What are the different Index Configurations a Table can have?

A table can have one of the following index configurations:

- No indexes
- A clustered index
- A clustered index and many non-clustered indexes
- A non-clustered index
- Many non-clustered indexes

What is the Filtered Index?

Filtered Index is used to index a portion of rows in a table that means it applies a filter on INDEX which improves query performance, reduces index maintenance costs, and reduces index storage costs when compared with full-table indexes. When we see an Index created with a WHERE clause, then that is a FILTERED INDEX.

What are Indexed Views inside SQL Server?

Views are a description of the data(metadata). When a view is a reference in the FROM clause its metadata is retrieved from the system catalog and placed into query. While working with a non-indexed view, the portion of the view is resolved at run time. In the case of the Index view, the view's result set is materialized immediately and persisted in physical storage in the database. During the run time this materialized storage is used to resolve the query result. Index view is primary created expecting performance improvement from the query which uses that index.

What are some of the restrictions of Indexed Views?

There are plenty of restrictions on the Indexed View. If Index is created on View the definition of the View must not contain any of the following:

- ANY, NOT ANY
- OPENROWSET, OPENQUERY, OPENDATASOURCE
- arithmetic on imprecise (float, real) values
- OPENXML
- COMPUTE, COMPUTE BY
- ORDER BY
- CONVERT producing an imprecise result
- OUTER join
- COUNT(*)
- reference to a base table with a disabled clustered index
- GROUP BY ALL (Read More Here)
- reference to a table or function in a different database
- Derived table (subquery in FROM list)
- reference to another view
- DISTINCT
- ROWSET function
- EXISTS, NOT EXISTS

- self-join
- expressions on aggregate results (e.g. SUM(x)+SUM(x))
- STDEV, STDEVP, VAR, VARP, AVG
- full-text predicates (CONTAINS, FREETEXT, CONTAINSTABLE, FREETEXTTABLE)
- Subquery
- imprecise constants (e.g. 2.34e5)
- SUM on nullable expressions
- inline or table-valued functions
- table hints (e.g. NOLOCK)
- MIN, MAX
- text, ntext, image, filestream, or XML columns
- non-deterministic expressions
- TOP
- non-unicode collations
- UNION
- contradictions SQL Server 2005 can detect that means the view would be empty (e.g. where 0=1 and ...)

What are DMVs and DMFs used for?

The DMVs (Dynamic Management Views) and DMFs (Dynamic Management Functions) are introduced in SQL Server 2005. It gives the database administrator information about the current state of the SQL Server machine in various aspects. From the basic definition, these dynamic management views and functions very much replace all the DBCC command outputs and the pseudo table outputs. Hence it is far easier to detect the health of SQL Server using these views and functions.

What are Statistics inside SQL Server?

Statistics are the heart and blood vein of the SQL Server Engine. Without Statistics, the SQL Server Engine cannot decide the most optimal execution plan for the query. Statistics are used for SELECT, INSERT, UPDATE and DELETE operations. It is very important to keep statistics updated for the server for an efficient low resource using an execution plan. You can check the statistics on any table using the following command.

```
USE AdventureWorks
GO
sp_helpstats 'Person.Contact';
GO
```

Section 3: Common Developer Questions

What is blocking?

SQL Server blocking occurs when one connection places a lock on a table (or selected rows, pages, extend) and another connection attempts to read or modify the data when the lock is in effect. Another connection has to wait till the resources are released from the original connection which is holding a lock on resources. Often blocking happens on the server where the system is under heavy transactional workload on a single resource. The way to resolve the blocking is to identify the statement which is creating blocking and optimize them (re-write T-SQL, Indexing, other configuration changes).

What is Deadlock? How can you identify/resolve a Deadlock?

Deadlocking occurs when two user processes have locks on separate objects and each process is trying to acquire a lock on the object that the other process has. In SQL Server when a Deadlock situation occurs it select the processes which have the least overhead to rollback to abort. This way deadlock is automatically resolved. There are multiple ways to identify deadlock i.e. Profile Deadlock Graph, DMV - sys.dm_tran_locks, Extended Events.

How is deadlock different from a blocking situation?

A deadlock occurs when two or more tasks permanently block each other by having a lock on a resource that the other tasks are trying to lock. In a deadlock situation, both transactions in the deadlock will wait forever unless the deadlock is broken while in a standard blocking scenario, the blocked task will simply wait until the blocking task releases the conflicting lock scenario.

What is the maximum row size for a table?

The maximum bytes per row is 8086 in SQL Server 2008 R2. Additionally, maximum bytes per varchar(max), varbinary(max), XML, text, or image column is 2GB (2^31-1). SQL Server 2005 and later version can handle more than 8086 bytes of the data by moving the record to another page in the ROW_OVERFLOW_DATA allocation unit. On the original page, it maintains a 24-byte pointer to this ROW_OVERFLOW_DATA allocation unit.

What are Sparse Columns?

A sparse column is another tool used to reduce the amount of physical storage used in a database. They are the ordinary columns that have optimized storage for null values. Sparse columns reduce the space requirements for null values at the cost of more overhead to retrieve non-null values.

What is XML Column-set with SPARSE Columns?

Tables that use sparse columns can designate a column to return all sparse columns in the table as an XML. A column set is like a calculated column in that the column set is not physically stored in the table. A column set differs from a calculated column in that the column set is directly updatable.

What is the maximum number of columns a table can have?

The maximum columns per table are 1024 in SQL Server 2008 R2 and later versions. If a table is a wide table which means it contains a SPARSE column, the columns per table is 30,000.

What have INCLUDED columns with SQL Server Indexes?

In SQL Server 2005 and later version, the functionality of non-clustered indexes is extended by adding non-key columns to the leaf level of the non-clustered index. Non-key columns can help to create cover indexes. By including non-key columns, you can create non-clustered indexes that cover more queries. The Database Engine does not consider non-key columns when calculating the number of index key columns or index key size. Non-key columns can be included in the non-clustered index to avoid exceeding the current index size limitations of a maximum of 16 key columns and a maximum index key size of 900 bytes. Another advantage is that using a non-key column in the index we can have index data types not allowed as index key columns generally.

What are the INTERSECT Operators?

INTERSECT operator in SQL Server 2005 and later version is used to retrieve the common records from both the left and the right query of the Intersect Operator. INTERSECT operator returns almost the same results as the INNER JOIN clause many times. When using INTERSECT operator the number and the order of the columns must be the same in all queries as well data type must be compatible.

What is Use of EXCEPT Clause?

EXCEPT clause is similar to the MINUS operation in Oracle. The EXCEPT query and MINUS query return all rows in the first query that are not returned in the second query. Each SQL statement within the EXCEPT query and MINUS query must have the same number of fields in the result sets with similar data types.

What are GROUPING SETS?

The GROUPING SETS, ROLLUP, and CUBE operators are added to the GROUP BY clause. Though the results can be mimicked by using UNION ALL operators, these new constructs are far more efficient. There is a new function, GROUPING_ID(), that returns more grouping-level information than the existing GROUPING() function. The non-ISO compliant WITH ROLLUP, WITH CUBE, and ALL syntax is deprecated.

What are Row Constructors inside SQL Server?

Transact-SQL is enhanced to allow multiple value inserts within a single INSERT statement. A simple construct is as follows –

```
INSERT INTO dbo.Persons (Name, Age)
VALUES ('Kumar', 35),
       ('Dave', 30)
```

What is the new Error Handling mechanism from SQL Server 2005?

SQL Server 2005 provides the TRY...CATCH construct, which is already present in many modern programming languages. TRY/CATCH helps to write logic separate the action and error handling code. The code meant for the action is enclosed in the TRY block and the code for error handling is enclosed in the CATCH block. In case the code within the TRY block fails, the control automatically jumps to the CATCH block, letting the transaction rollback and resume execution. In addition to this, the CATCH block captures and provides error information that shows you the ID, message text, state, severity and transaction state of an error.

What is an OUTPUT Clause inside SQL Server?

SQL Server 2005 has a new OUTPUT clause, which is quite useful. OUTPUT clause has accesses to inserted and deleted tables (virtual tables) just like triggers. OUTPUT clause can be used to return values to the client clause. OUTPUT clause can be used with INSERT, UPDATE, or DELETE to identify the actual rows affected by these statements. OUTPUT clause can generate a table variable, a permanent table, or a temporary table. Even though @@Identity will still work in SQL Server 2005, however, I find the OUTPUT clause very easy and powerful to use. Let us understand the OUTPUT clause using an example.

What are Table Valued Parameters?

Table-Valued Parameter is a new feature introduced in SQL SERVER. In earlier versions of SQL SERVER, it is not possible to pass a table variable in a stored procedure as a parameter, but now in SQL SERVER, we can use Table-Valued Parameter to send multiple rows of data to a stored procedure or a function without creating a temporary table or passing so many parameters. Table-valued parameters are declared using user-defined table types. To use Table-Valued Parameters we need to follow the steps shown below:

- Create a table type and define the table structure
- Declare a stored procedure that has a parameter of table type.
- Declare a table type variable and reference the table type.
- Using the INSERT statement and occupy the variable.
- We can now pass the variable to the procedure.

What is the use of Data-Tier Application (DACPAC)?

The need for a data-tier application is to simplify the development, deployment, and management of the database/data-tier objects that support a multi-tier or client-server application. DACPAC defines all of the Database Engine schema and instance objects, such as tables, views, and logins, required to support the application. The DAC operates as a single unit of management through the development, deployment, and management lifecycle of the associated application. The DAC also contains policies that define the deployment prerequisites for the DAC.

What is RAID?

RAID (redundant array of independent disks) is a way of storing the same data in different places on multiple hard disks. By placing data on multiple disks, input/output operations can overlap in a balanced way, improving performance. Following are a few popular RAID types configuration used for Database Storage.

- RAID 0 – No Redundancy
- RAID 1 – Mirroring
- RAID 5 – Distributed Parity
- RAID 10 - Mirrored and Striped

What are the Properties and Different Types of Sub-Queries?

Properties of a Sub-Query

- A sub-query must be enclosed in the parenthesis.
- A sub-query must be put on the right hand of the comparison operator, and
- A sub-query cannot contain an ORDER BY clause.
- A query can contain more than one sub-query.

Types of Sub-query

- Single-row sub-query, where the subquery returns only one row.
- Multiple-row sub-query, where the subquery returns multiple rows, and
- Multiple column sub-query, where the sub-query returns multiple columns

What are PIVOT and UNPIVOT?

A Pivot Table can automatically sort, count, and total the data stored in one table or spreadsheet and create a second table displaying the summarized data. The PIVOT operator turns the values of a specified column into column names, effectively rotating a table.
UNPIVOT table is reverse of PIVOT Table.

Can a Stored Procedure call itself or a Recursive Stored Procedure? How many levels of SP nesting is possible?

Yes. As T-SQL supports recursion, you can write stored procedures that call themselves. Recursion can be defined as a method of problem-solving wherein the solution is arrived at by repetitively applying it to subsets of the problem. A common application of recursive logic is to perform numeric computations that lend themselves to repetitive evaluation by the same processing steps. Stored procedures are nested when one stored procedure calls another or executes managed code by referencing a CLR routine, type, or aggregate. You can nest stored procedures and managed code references up to 32 levels.

Section 4: Common Tricky Questions

Which TCP/IP port does the SQL Server run on? How can it be Changed?

SQL Server runs on port 1433. It can be changed from the SQL Server Configuration Manager -> SQL Server Network Configurations -> Protocols for SQL Server -> TCP/IP properties –> IP Addresses -> TCP Port number, both on the client and the server.

What is the difference between Clustered and a Non-clustered Index?

A clustered index is a special type of index that reorders the way records in the table are physically stored. Therefore, the table can have only one clustered index. The leaf nodes of a clustered index contain the actual data.

A non-clustered index is a special type of index in which the logical order of the index does not match the physical stored order of the rows on the disk. The leaf node of a non-clustered index does not consist of the data pages. Instead, the leaf nodes contain index rows and a pointer to data (Clustered Index key or RID).

When is the use of the UPDATE_STATISTICS command?

This command is used when a large amount of data is processed. If a large amount of deletions, modifications or Bulk Copy into the tables has occurred, it has to update the indexes to take these changes into account. UPDATE_STATISTICS updates the indexes on these tables accordingly.

What is an SQL Profiler?

SQL Profiler is a graphical tool that allows system administrators to monitor events in an instance of Microsoft SQL Server. You can capture and save data about each event to a file or SQL Server table to analyze later. For example, you can monitor a production environment to see which stored procedures are hampering performances by executing very slowly.

Use SQL Profiler to monitor only the events in which you are interested. If traces are becoming too large, you can filter them based on the information you want, so that only a subset of the event data is collected. Monitoring too many events adds overhead to the server and the monitoring process and can cause the trace file or trace table to grow very large, especially when the monitoring process takes place over a long period.

What is an SQL Server Agent?

The SQL Server agent plays an important role in the day-to-day tasks of a database administrator (DBA). It is often overlooked as one of the main tools for SQL Server management. Its purpose is to ease the implementation of tasks for the DBA, with its full-function scheduling engine, which allows you to schedule your jobs and scripts.

What is BCP? When is it Used?

BCP or BulkCopy is a tool used to copy huge amounts of data from tables and views. BCP does not copy the complete structures from source to destination. BULK INSERT command helps to import a data file into a database table or view it in a user-specified format.

What are the Authentication Modes in SQL Server? How can it be Changed?

There are two authentication modes in SQL Server.

- Windows Mode
- Mixed Mode – SQL and Windows

To change authentication mode in SQL Server, go to Start -> Programs- > Microsoft SQL Server and click SQL Server Management Studio and under *Object Explorer*, right-click the server, and then click *Properties*. On the *Security page*, under Server authentication, select the new server authentication mode, and then click OK.

Can you have SQL Server without a SA account?

The SA account is a well-known guessable SQL Server account and is often targeted by malicious users. Do not enable the SA account unless your application requires it. With SQL Server 2008 R2 onwards, you can also rename the SA account. If Windows Authentication mode is selected during installation, the sa login is disabled and a password is assigned by setup. If you later change authentication mode to SQL Server and Windows Authentication mode, the sa login remains disabled.

Which Command using SQL Server Management Studio will give you the version of SQL Server and Operating System?

```
SELECT SERVERPROPERTY('Edition') AS Edition,
SERVERPROPERTY('ProductLevel') AS ProductLevel,
SERVERPROPERTY('ProductVersion') AS ProductVersion
GO
```

What is Log Shipping?

Log shipping is the process of automating the backup of database and transaction log files on a production SQL server and then restoring them onto a standby server. In log shipping, the transactional log file from one server is automatically updated into the backup database on the other server. If one server fails, the other server will have the same DB and can be used as the Disaster Recovery plan. The key feature of log shipping is that it will automatically backup transaction logs throughout the day and automatically restore them on the standby server at defined intervals.

Name a few ways to get an Accurate Count of the Number of Records in a Table?

```
SELECT * FROM table1;

SELECT COUNT(*) FROM table1;
```

```
SELECT rows FROM sysindexes
WHERE id = OBJECT_ID(table1) AND indid < 2
```

Using SQL Server 2008 and later version DMVs:

```
SELECT object_name(i.object_id) as objectName, i.[name] as
indexName, sum(p.rows) as rowCnt
FROM sys.indexes I
INNER JOIN sys.partitions p
  ON i.object_id = p.object_id AND i.index_id = p.index_id
WHERE i.object_id = object_id('dbo.table1')
  AND i.index_id <= 1
GROUP BY i.object_id, i.index_id, i.[name]
```

What does it mean to have QUOTED_IDENTIFIER ON? What are the implications of having it OFF?

When SET QUOTED_IDENTIFIER is ON, identifiers can be delimited by double quotation marks, and literals must be delimited by single quotation marks. When SET QUOTED_IDENTIFIER is OFF, identifiers cannot be quoted and must follow all T-SQL rules for identifiers.

What is the difference between a Local and a Global Temporary Table?

A local temporary table exists only for the duration of a connection, or if defined inside a compound statement, for the duration of the compound statement.

A global temporary table remains in the database permanently, but the rows exist only within a given connection. When the connection is closed, the data in the global temporary table disappears. However, the table definition remains with the database for access when a database is opened next time.

What Table variables and how are they different from Local Temporary tables?

A Table variable is like a Local temporary table but has some interesting differences. The scoping rules of Table variables are the same as any other variable inside SQL Server. For example, if you define a variable inside a stored procedure, it can't be accessed outside the stored procedure.

- The table variable is NOT necessarily a memory resident. Under memory pressure, the pages belonging to a table variable can be pushed out to tempdb.
- Rollback doesn't affect table variables, unlike Temp tables. Table variables don't participate in transactions or locking.
- Any DML operations done on Table variables are NOT logged.
- No statistics are maintained for the table variable which means - any changes in data impacting the table variable will not cause recompilation of queries accessing the table variable.

What is the STUFF Function and How Does it Differ from the REPLACE Function?

STUFF function is used to overwrite existing characters using this syntax: STUFF (string_expression, start, length, replacement_characters), where string_expression is the string that will have characters substituted, the start is the starting position, the length is the number of characters in the string that are substituted, and replacement_characters are the new characters interjected into the string. REPLACE function is used to replace existing characters of all occurrences. Using the syntax REPLACE (string_expression, search_string, replacement_string), every incidence of search_string found in the string_expression will be replaced with replacement_string.

How to get @@ERROR and @@ROWCOUNT at the Same Time?

If @@Rowcount is checked after the error-checking statement, then it will have 0 as the value of @@Recordcount as it would have been reset. And if @@Recordcount is checked before the error-checking statement, then @@Error would get reset. To get @@error and @@rowcount at the same time, include both in the same statement and store them in a local variable. SELECT @RC = @@ROWCOUNT, @ER = @@ERROR

What is a Scheduled Job or What is a Scheduled Task?

Scheduled task lets administrators automate processes that run on regular or predictable cycles as part of maintenance. User can schedule administrative tasks, such as cube processing, to run during times of slow business activity. User can also determine the order in which tasks run by creating job steps within a SQL Server Agent job, e.g. back up the database and update statistics of the tables. Job steps give the user control over the flow of execution. If one job fails, then the user can configure SQL Server Agent to continue to run the remaining tasks or to stop the execution.

What are the Advantages of Using Stored Procedures?

- A stored procedure can reduce network traffic and latency, boosting application performance.
- Stored procedure execution plans can be reused; they staying cached in SQL Server's memory, reducing server overhead.
- Stored procedures help promote code reuse.
- Stored procedures can encapsulate logic. You can change the stored procedure code without affecting clients.
- Stored procedures provide better security to your data.

What is a Table Called, if it has neither Cluster nor Non-cluster Index?

Unindexed table or Heap. Microsoft Press Books and Book on Line (BOL) refers to it as Heap. A heap is a table that does not have a clustered index and therefore, the pages are not linked by pointers. The IAM pages are the only structures that link the pages in a table together. Unindexed tables are good for the fast storing of data. Many times, it is better to drop all the indexes from the table and then do the bulk of INSERTs and restore those indexes after that.

Can SQL Server be linked to other servers like Oracle?

SQL Server can be linked to any server provided it has an OLE-DB provider from Microsoft to allow a link, e.g. Oracle has an OLE-DB provider that Microsoft provides to add it as a linked server to the SQL Server group.

What Command do we Use to Rename a DB, a Table and a Column?

To Rename DB

sp_renamedb 'oldname' , 'newname'

If someone is using DB it will not accept sp_renmaedb. In that case, first, bring DB to single-user mode using sp_dboptions. Use sp_renamedb to rename the database. Use sp_dboptions to bring the database to multi-user mode.

e.g.

```
USE master;
GO
EXEC sp_dboption AdventureWorks, 'Single User', True
GO
EXEC sp_renamedb 'AdventureWorks', 'AdventureWorks_New'
GO
EXEC sp_dboption AdventureWorks, 'Single User', False
GO
```

To Rename Table

We can change the table name using sp_rename as follows:

sp_rename 'oldTableName' 'newTableName'

e.g.

```
SP_RENAME 'Table_First', 'Table_Last'
GO
```

To rename Column

The script for renaming any column is as follows:

sp_rename 'TableName.[OldcolumnName]', 'NewColumnName', 'Column'

e.g.

```
sp_RENAME 'Table_First.Name', 'NameChange' , 'COLUMN'
GO
```

What are sp_configure Commands and SET Commands?

Use sp_configure to display or change server-level settings. To change the database-level settings, use ALTER DATABASE. To change settings that affect only the current user session, use the SET statement.

e.g.

```
sp_CONFIGURE 'show advanced', 0
GO
RECONFIGURE
```

```
GO
sp_CONFIGURE
GO
```

You can run the following command and check the advanced global configuration settings.

```
sp_CONFIGURE 'show advanced', 1
GO
RECONFIGURE
GO
sp_CONFIGURE
GO
```

How to Implement One-to-One, One-to-Many and Many-to-Many Relationships while Designing Tables?

A one-to-one relationship can be implemented as a single table and rarely as two tables with primary and foreign key relationships. One-to-Many relationships are implemented by splitting the data into two tables with primary key and foreign key relationships. Many-to-Many relationships are implemented using a junction table with the keys from both the tables forming the composite primary key of the junction table.

What is the Difference between Commit and Rollback when Used in Transactions?

The usual structure of the TRANSACTION is as follows:

```
BEGIN TRANSACTION
    <<Procedural / SET Operations>>
COMMIT TRANSACTION or ROLLBACK TRANSACTION
```

When Commit is executed, every statement between BEGIN TRANSACTION and COMMIT becomes persistent to the database. When Rollback is executed, every statement between BEGIN TRANSACTION and ROLLBACK are reverted to the state when the BEGIN TRANSACTION was executed.

What is an Execution Plan? When would you use it? How would you View the Execution Plan?

An execution plan is a road map graphically or textually representation of data retrieval methods chosen by the SQL Server query optimizer for a stored procedure or ad-hoc query, and it is a very useful tool for a developer to understand the performance characteristics of a query or stored procedure since the plan is the one that SQL Server will place in its cache and use to execute the stored procedure or query. Within the SQL Server Management Studio, there is an option called "Include Actual Execution Plan" (or use CTRL+M shortcut) under the SQL Editor Toolbar. If this option is turned on, it will display the query execution plan in a separate window when the query is executed.

What is CHECKPOINT Process in the SQL Server?

CHECKPOINT process writes all in-memory dirty pages for the current database to disk. Dirty pages are data pages that have been entered into the buffer cache and modified but not yet written to disk. Checkpoints save time during a later recovery by creating a point at which all dirty pages are guaranteed to have been written to disk.

What is the Difference between Table Aliases and Column Aliases? Do they Affect Performance?

Usually, when the name of the table or column is very long or complicated to write, aliases are used to refer to them.

e.g.

```
SELECT VeryLongColumnName col1
FROM VeryLongTableName tab1
```

In the above example, col1 and tab1 are the column alias and table alias, respectively. They do not affect the performance at all.

What is the difference between CHAR and VARCHAR Datatypes?

VARCHARS are variable-length strings with a specified maximum length. If a string is less than the maximum length, then it is stored verbatim without any extra characters, e.g. names and emails. CHARS are fixed-length strings with a specified set length. If a string is less than the set length, then it is padded with extra characters, e.g. phone number and zip codes. For instance, for a column that is declared as VARCHAR(30) and populated with the word 'SQL Server,' only 10 bytes will be stored in it. However, if we have declared the column as CHAR(30) and populated it with the word 'SQL Server,' it will still occupy 30 bytes in the database.

What is the difference between VARCHAR and VARCHAR(MAX) Datatypes?

VARCHAR stores variable-length character data whose range varies up to 8000 bytes; varchar(MAX) stores variable-length character data whose range may vary beyond 8000 bytes and till 2 GB. TEXT datatype and "Text in row" table option will be deprecated in future versions, and the usage of VARCHAR(MAX) is strongly recommended instead of TEXT datatypes. VARCHAR(MAX) Datatypes can be used inside triggers and unlike Text, datatype can be used with normal string functions (LEN, Substring, Concatenation, as Local variables etc).

What is the difference between VARCHAR and NVARCHAR datatypes?

In principle, they are the same and are handled in the same way by your application. The only difference is that NVARCHAR can handle Unicode characters, allowing you to use multiple languages in the database (Arabian, Chinese etc.). NVARCHAR takes twice as much space when compared to VARCHAR. Use NVARCHAR only if you need localization or internationalization support.

Which are the Important Points to Note when Multilanguage Data is Stored in a Table?

There are two things to keep in mind while storing Unicode data. First, the column must be of Unicode data type (nchar, nvarchar, ntext). Second, the value must be prefixed with N while insertion. For example,

```
INSERT INTO table (Hindi_col) values (N'हिंदी data')
```

How to Optimize Stored Procedure Optimization?

There are many tips and tricks for the same. Here are a few:

- Include SET NOCOUNT ON statement.
- Use the schema name with the object name.
- Do not use the prefix "sp_" in the stored procedure name.
- Use IF EXISTS (SELECT 1) instead of (SELECT *).
- Use the sp_executesql stored procedure instead of the EXECUTE statement for Dynamic SQLs.
- Try to avoid using SQL Server cursors whenever possible.
- Keep the Transaction as short as possible.
- Use TRY-Catch for error handling.
- Optimize queries and fine-tune indexes.
- Use table variables and temp tables appropriately.

What is SQL Injection? How to Protect Against SQL Injection Attack?

SQL injection is an attack in which malicious code is inserted into strings that are later passed to an instance of SQL Server for parsing and execution. Any procedure that constructs SQL statements should be reviewed for injection vulnerabilities because SQL Server will execute all syntactically valid queries that it receives. Even parameterized data can be manipulated by a skilled and determined attacker.

Here are a few methods which can be used to protect again SQL Injection attack:

- Use Type-Safe SQL Parameters
- Use Parameterized Input with Stored Procedures
- Use the Parameters Collection with Dynamic SQL
- Use the escape character in the LIKE clause
- Wrapping Parameters with QUOTENAME() and REPLACE()
- Validate ALL input elements. For unstructured data like XML documents, validate all data against a schema as it is entered.
- Never concatenate user input that is not validated. String concatenation is the primary point of entry for script injection.
- Always run the SPs under Least privileges to DB. Deny direct access to DB objects.

How to Find Out the List Schema Name and Table Name for the Database?

We can use any of the following scripts:

```
SELECT '['+SCHEMA_NAME(schema_id)+'].['+ Name +']' AS SchemaTable
```

```
FROM sys.tables

SELECT '['+ TABLE_SCHEMA +'].['+ TABLE_NAME +']' AS SchemaTable
FROM INFORMATION_SCHEMA.TABLES
```

How does using a Separate Hard Drive for Several Database Objects Improves Performance Right Away?

Separating objects across different physical Hard drives will increase the number of IOPS that can be handled in parallel for the SQL Server instance. This is a deployment strategy done by the DBA. A non-clustered index and tempdb can be created on a separate disk to improve performance.

How to Find the List of Fixed Hard Drive and Free Space on Server?

We can use the following Stored Procedure to figure out the number of fixed drives (hard drive) a system has along with free space on each of those drives.

```
EXEC master..xp_fixeddrives
```

Why can there be only one Clustered Index and not more than one?

A clustered index determines the physical order of data in a table. As a fact, we all know that a set of data can be only stored in only one physical order; that is why only one clustered index is possible.

What is the difference between Line Feed (\n) and Carriage Return (\r)?

Line Feed – LF – \n – 0x0a – 10 (decimal)
Carriage Return – CR – \r – 0x0D – 13 (decimal)

```
DECLARE @NewLineChar AS CHAR(2) = CHAR(13) + CHAR(10)
PRINT ('SELECT FirstLine AS FL ' +@NewLineChar + 'SELECT SecondLine AS SL' )
```

What is a Hint?

Hints are options and strong suggestions specified for enforcement by the SQL Server query processor on DML statements. The hints override any execution plan the query optimizer might select for a query.

There are three different types of hints. Let us understand the basics of each of them separately.

Join Hint

This hint is used when more than one table is used in a query. Two or more tables can be joined using different types of joins. This hint forces the type of join algorithm (INNER [LOOP | MERGE | JOIN] JOIN) that is used. Joins can be used in SELECT, UPDATE and DELETE statements.

Query Hint

This hint is used when a certain kind of logic has to be applied to a whole query. Any hint used in the query is applied to the complete query as opposed to a part of it. There is no way to specify that only a certain part of a query should be used with the hint. After any query, the OPTION clause is specified to apply the logic to this query. A query always has any of the following statements: SELECT, UPDATE, DELETE, INSERT or MERGE (SQL 2008); and this hint can be applied to all of them.

Table Hint

This hint is used when a certain kind of locking mechanism of tables has to be controlled. SQL Server query optimizer always puts the appropriate kind of lock on tables, when any of the Transact SQL operations SELECT, UPDATE, DELETE, INSERT or MERGE is used. There are certain cases when the developer knows when and where to override the default behaviour of the locking algorithm, and these hints are useful in those scenarios.

How to Delete Duplicate Rows?

We can delete duplicate rows using the CTE and ROW_NUMBER () feature of SQL Server 2005 and SQL Server 2008.

e.g.

```
WITH CTE (COl1,Col2, DuplicateCount)
AS
(
SELECT COl1,Col2,
ROW_NUMBER() OVER(PARTITION BY COl1,Col2 ORDER BY Col1) AS DuplicateCount
FROM DuplicateRcordTable
)
DELETE
FROM CTE
WHERE DuplicateCount >1
```

Why the LOGON Trigger Fires Multiple Times in Single Login?

It happens because multiple SQL Server services are running and also as SQL Server Management Studio Intellisense is turned on. If you are having the Object Explorer open apart from the Query window, then these also open connections to SQL Server that gets logged.

What are Aggregate Functions?

Aggregate functions perform a calculation on a set of values and return a single value. Aggregate functions ignore NULL values except for the COUNT function. HAVING clause is used, along with GROUP BY for filtering query using aggregate values.

The following functions are some of the aggregate functions.

AVG, MIN, CHECKSUM_AGG, SUM, COUNT, STDEV, COUNT_BIG, STDEVP, GROUPING, VAR, MAX, VARP

What is the Use of @@ SPID in SQL Server?

A SPID is the SQL Server session ID of the current user connection. And using that session ID, we can find out that the last query was executed.

What is the difference between the Index Seek vs. Index Scan?

An index scan means that SQL Server reads all rows in a table, and then returns only those rows that satisfy the search criteria. When an index scan is performed, all the rows in the leaf level of the index are scanned. This essentially means that all the rows of the index are examined instead of the table directly. This is sometimes compared to a table scan, in which all the table data is read directly. However, there is usually little difference between an index scan and a table scan.

An index seeks, on the other hand, means that the Query Optimizer relies entirely on the index leaf data to locate rows satisfying the query condition. An index seek will be most beneficial in cases where a small percentage (less than 10 or 15 percentage) of rows will be returned. An index seek will only affect the rows that satisfy a query condition and the pages that contain these qualifying rows; in terms of performance, this is highly beneficial when a table has a very large number of rows.

What is the Maximum Size per Database for SQL Server Express?

SQL Server Express supports a maximum size of 4 GB per database, which excludes all the log files. From SQL Server 2008 R2 onwards this size has been made to 10GB. This is quite some data for a conventional application and when designed properly can be used efficiently for small development purposes.

How do We Know if Any Query is Retrieving Large or very little data?

In one way, it is quite easy to figure this out by just looking at the result set; however, this method cannot rely upon every time as it is difficult to reach a conclusion when there are many columns and many rows.

It is easy to measure how much data is retrieved from the server to the client-side. The SQL Server Management Studio has a feature that can measure client statistics.

How to Create Primary Key with a Specific Name while Creating a Table?

```
CREATE TABLE [dbo].[TestTable](
[ID] [int] IDENTITY(1,1)NOT NULL,
[FirstName] [varchar](100)NULL,
CONSTRAINT [PK_TestTable] PRIMARY KEY CLUSTERED
([ID] ASC))
GO
```

What is T-SQL Script to Take Database Offline – Take Database Online?

```
-- Take the Database Offline
ALTER DATABASE [myDB] SET OFFLINE WITH
ROLLBACK IMMEDIATE
GO
```

```
-- Take the Database Online
ALTER DATABASE [myDB] SET ONLINE
GO
```

Can we Insert Data if Clustered Index is Disabled?

No, we cannot insert data if the Clustered Index is disabled because Clustered Indexes are original tables that are physically ordered according to one or more keys (Columns).

How to Recompile Stored Procedure at Run Time?

We can Recompile Stored Procedure in two ways.

Option 1:

```
CREATE PROCEDURE dbo.PersonAge(@MinAge INT, @MaxAge INT)
WITH RECOMPILE
AS
SELECT*
FROM dbo.tblPerson
WHERE Age >= @MinAge AND Age <= @MaxAge
GO
```

Option 2:

```
EXEC dbo.PersonAge65, 70 WITH RECOMPILE
```

We can use the RECOMPILE hint with a query and recompile only that particular query. However, if the parameters are used in many statements in the stored procedure and we want to recompile all the statements, then instead of using the RECOMPILE option with all the queries, we have one better option that uses WITH RECOMPILE during stored procedure creation or execution.

This method is not recommended for large stored procedures because the recompilation of so many statements may outweigh the benefit of a better execution plan.

Describe the performance difference between IF EXISTS (Select null from table) and IF EXISTS (Select 1 from table).

When you write select null, it will still return 4 bytes of memory on a 32-bit machine for the return value. And when you are returning 1 byte or 2 bytes, you end up taking 4 bytes of memory because of the padding to keep memory aligned.
So there is no performance difference between IF EXISTS (Select null from table) and IF EXISTS (Select 1 from table).

What is the difference in Performance between INSERT TOP (N) INTO Table and Using Top with INSERT?

INSERT TOP (N) INTO Table is faster than Using Top with INSERT but when we use INSERT TOP (N) INTO Table, the ORDER BY clause is ignored.

Does the Order of Columns in UPDATE statements Matter?

No, the order of columns in UPDATE statement does not matter. Both the below options produce the same results.

Option 1:

```
UPDATE TableName
SET Col1 ='Value', Col2 ='Value2'
```

Option 2:

```
UPDATE TableName
SET Col2 ='Value2', Col1 ='Value'
```

Section 5: Miscellaneous Questions on SQL SERVER

What are the basic functions for master, msdb, model, tempdb and resource databases?

*The **master** database* holds information for all the databases located on the SQL Server instance, and it is the glue that holds the engine together. Because SQL Server cannot start without a functioning master database, you must administer this database with care.

*The **msdb** database* stores information regarding database backups, SQL Agent information, DTS packages, SQL Server jobs, PBM information and some replication information such as for log shipping.

*The **tempdb*** holds temporary objects such as global and local temporary tables and is a very important database for the instance. It is also the database that stores the version store when Snapshot Isolations are used. Each time SQL Server restarts tempdb is copied from the model database.

*The **model*** is essentially a template database used in the creation of any new user database created in the instance.

*The **resource** database* is a read-only database that contains all the system objects that are included in the SQL Server. SQL Server system objects such as sys.objects are physically persisted in the Resource database, but they logically appear in the sys schema of every database. The Resource database does not contain user data or user metadata.

What is the Maximum Number of Index per Table?

Till SQL Server 2005:
1 Clustered Index + 249 Nonclustered Index = 250 Index.

For SQL Server 2008 onwards:
1 Clustered Index + 999 Nonclustered Index = 1000 Index.

Explain a few of the New Features of SQL Server 2008 Management Studio

SQL Server 2008 Microsoft has upgraded SSMS with many new features as well as added tons of new functionalities requested by DBAs for a long time. A few of the important new features are as follows:

- IntelliSense for Query Editing
- Multi-Server Query
- Query Editor Regions
- Object Explorer Enhancements
- Activity Monitors

Explain IntelliSense for Query Editing:

After implementing IntelliSense, we don't have to remember all the syntax or browse online references. IntelliSense offers a few additional features besides just completing the keyword and giving options for object names to complete the query.

Explain MultiServer Query:

SSMS 2008 has a feature to run a query on different servers from one query editor window. First of all, make sure that you registered all the servers under your registered server. Once they are registered, right-click on the server group name and click New Query.

e.g. for server version information,

```
SELECT
SERVERPROPERTY('Edition') AS Edition,
SERVERPROPERTY('ProductLevel') AS ProductLevel,
SERVERPROPERTY('ProductVersion') AS ProductVersion
```

Explain Query Editor Regions:

When the T-SQL code is more than hundreds of lines, after a while, it becomes more and more confusing. The regions are defined by the following hierarchy:
From the first GO command to the next GO command.
Statements between BEGIN – END, BEGIN TRY – END TRY, BEGIN CATCH – END CATCH.

Explain Object Explorer Enhancements:

In Object Explorer Detail, the new feature is Object Search. Enter any object name in the object search box and the searched result will be displayed in the same window as Object Explorer Detail.

Additionally, there are new wizards which help you perform several tasks, from policy management to disk monitoring. One cool thing is that everything displayed in the object explorer details screen can be right away copied and pasted to Excel without any formatting issue.

Explain Activity Monitors:

There are four graphs

- percent; Processor Time,
- Waiting Tasks,
- Database I/O,
- Batch Requests/Sec

All the four tabs provide very important information; however, the one which I prefer most is "Recent Expensive Queries." Whenever I find my server running slow or having any performance-related issues, my first reaction is to open this tab and see which query is running slow. I usually look at the query with the highest number for Average

Duration. The Recent Expensive Queries monitors only show queries that are in the SQL Server cache at that moment.

What is Service Broker?

Service Broker is a message-queuing technology in SQL Server that allows developers to integrate SQL Server fully into distributed applications. Service Broker is a feature that provides a facility to SQL Server to send an asynchronous, transactional message. It allows a database to send a message to another database without waiting for the response; so the application will continue to function if the remote database is temporarily unavailable.

What does TOP Operator Do?

The TOP operator is used to specify the number of rows to be returned by a query. The TOP operator has a new addition in SQL SERVER 2008 that it accepts variables as well as literal values and can be used with INSERT, UPDATE, and DELETES statements.

What is CTE?

CTE is the abbreviation for *Common Table Expression.* A CTE is an expression that can be thought of as a temporary result set that is defined within the execution of a single SQL statement. A CTE is similar to a derived table in that it is not stored as an object and lasts only for the duration of the query.

A CTE can reference itself, thereby creating a recursive CTE. A recursive CTE is one in which an initial CTE is repeatedly executed to return subsets of data until the complete result set is obtained. A recursive CTE contains 3 elements –

- An initializer – this is like the data to start
- Recursive part – this is where the initializer feeds the data for recursion
- Termination – defines when the recursion must end

What are some advantages of using CTE?

- Using CTE improves the readability and enables easy maintenance of complex queries.
- The query can be divided into separate, simple, and logical building blocks, which can be then used to build more complex CTEs until the final result set is generated.
- CTE make writing recursive code in T-SQL significantly easier than it was in previous versions of SQL Server.
- CTE can be defined in functions, stored procedures, triggers or even views.
- After a CTE is defined, it can be used as a Table or a View and can SELECT, INSERT, UPDATE or DELETE Data.

How can we Rewrite Sub-Queries into Simple Select Statements or with Joins?

Yes. We can rewrite sub-queries using the Common Table Expression (CTE). A Common Table Expression (CTE) is an expression that can be thought of as a temporary result set that is defined within the execution of a single SQL statement. A CTE is similar to a derived table in that it is not stored as an object and lasts only for the duration of the query.

e.g.

```
USE AdventureWorks
GO
WITH EmployeeDepartment_CTE AS (
        SELECT EmployeeID,DepartmentID,ShiftID
        FROM HumanResources.EmployeeDepartmentHistory
)
SELECT ecte.EmployeeId, ed.DepartmentID, ed.Name,ecte.ShiftID
FROM HumanResources.Department ed
INNER JOIN EmployeeDepartment_CTE ecte
ON ecte.DepartmentID = ed.DepartmentID
GO
```

What is the MERGE Statement?

MERGE is a new feature that provides an efficient way to perform multiple DML operations in a single statement. In previous versions of SQL Server, we had to write separate statements to INSERT, UPDATE, or DELETE data based on certain conditions, but now, using MERGE statement, we can include the logic of such data modifications in one statement that even checks when the data is matched, then just update it, and when unmatched, insert it. One of the most important advantages of the MERGE statement is all the data is read and processed only once.

Which are the New Data Types Introduced in SQL SERVER 2008?

The GEOMETRY Type: The GEOMETRY data type is a system .NET common language runtime (CLR) datatype in SQL Server. This type represents data in a two-dimensional Euclidean coordinate system.

The GEOGRAPHY Type: The GEOGRAPHY datatype's functions are the same as with GEOMETRY. The difference between the two is that when you specify GEOGRAPHY, you are usually specifying points in terms of latitude and longitude.

New Date and Time Data types: SQL Server 2008 introduces four new data types related to date and time: DATE, TIME, DATETIMEOFFSET, and DATETIME2.

- DATE: The new DATE data type just stores the data itself. It is based on the Gregorian calendar and handles years from 1 to 9999.
- TIME: The new TIME (*n*) type stores time with a range of 00:00:00.0000000 through 23:59:59.9999999. Precision is allowed with this type. TIME supports seconds down to 100 nanoseconds. The *n* in TIME(*n*) defines this level of fractional second precision from 0 to 7 digits of precision.
- The DATETIMEOFFSET Type: DATETIMEOFFSET (*n*) is the time-zone-aware version of a datetime datatype. The name will appear less odd when you consider what it

is: a date + time + time-zone offset. The offset is based on how far behind or ahead you are from Coordinated Universal Time (UTC) time.

- The DATETIME2 Type: It is an extension of the datetime type in earlier versions of SQL Server. This new datatype has a date range covering dates from January 1 of year 1 through December 31 of year 9999. DATETIME2 not only includes the larger date range but also has a timestamp and the same fractional precision that TIME type provides.

What is CLR?

In SQL Server 2008, SQL Server objects such as user-defined functions can be created using such CLR languages. This CLR language support extends not only to user-defined functions but also to stored procedures and triggers. You can develop such CLR add-ons to SQL Server using Visual Studio.

Define HIERARCHYID Datatypes?

The new HIERARCHYID data type in SQL Server 2008 is a system-supplied CLR UDT that can be useful for storing and manipulating hierarchies. It is internally stored as a VARBINARY that represents the position of the current node in the hierarchy. You can create indexes, query nodes, add siblings etc just like any other data inside SQL Server.

What are Table Types and Table-Valued Parameters?

SQL Server 2008 introduces these concepts. *Table types* save a table definition in the database and can be used later to define table variables or parameters. Because table types let you reuse a table definition, they ensure consistency and reduce chances for errors.

We can now use table types as the types for input parameters of stored procedures and functions hence are called *Table-Valued Parameters* (TVP). A common scenario where TVPs are very useful is passing an "array" of keys to a stored procedure.

What are Synonyms?

Synonyms give you the ability to provide alternate names for database objects. You can alias object names; for example, using the Employee table as Emp. You can also shorten names. This is especially useful when dealing with three and four-part names; for example, shortening server.database.owner.object to object.

What is LINQ?

Language-Integrated Query (LINQ) adds the ability to query objects using .NET languages. The LINQ to SQL object/relational mapping (O/RM) framework provides the following basic features:

- Tools to create classes (usually called *entities*) mapped to database tables
- Compatibility with LINQ's standard query operations
- The DataContext class with features such as entity record monitoring, automatic SQL statement generation, record concurrency detection, and much more

What are Isolation Levels?

Transactions specify an isolation level that defines the degree to which one transaction must be isolated from resource or data modifications made by other transactions. Isolation levels are described in terms of which concurrency side-effects, such as dirty reads or phantom reads, are allowed.

Transaction isolation levels control the following:

- Whether locks are taken when data is read, and what type of locks are requested.
- How long the read locks are held.
- Whether a read operation referencing rows modified by another transaction
  - blocks until the exclusive lock on the row are freed,
  - retrieves the committed version of the row that existed at the time the statement or transaction started, and
    - reads the uncommitted data modification.

How will you Handle Error in SQL SERVER 2008?

SQL Server now supports the use of TRY...CATCH constructs for providing rich error handling. TRY...CATCH lets us build error handling at the level we need, in the way we need to by setting a region where if any error occurs, it will break out of the region and head to an error handler. The basic structure is as follows:

```
BEGIN TRY
<code>
END TRY
BEGIN CATCH
<code>
END CATCH
```

What are some of the salient behaviours of the TRY...CATCH block?

When an error condition is detected in a TSQL statement that is inside a TRY block, control is passed to a CATCH block where the error can be processed.

- If there are no errors inside the TRY block, control passes to the statement immediately after the associated END CATCH statement.
- A TRY block must be followed immediately by a CATCH block.
- Each TRY block is associated with only one CATCH block.
- Each TRY...CATCH construct must be inside a single batch. We cannot place a TRY block in one batch and the associated CATCH block in another batch.
- TRY...CATCH constructs can be nested.
- ERROR_PROCEDURE() returns the name of the stored procedure or trigger where the error occurred.
-

What is RAISEERROR?

RAISERROR generates an error message and initiates error processing for the session. RAISERROR can either reference a user-defined message stored in the **sys.messages** catalog view or build a message dynamically. The message is returned as a server error message to the calling application or an associated CATCH block of a TRY...CATCH construct.

What is the XML Datatype?

The **XML** data type lets you store XML documents and fragments in a SQL Server database. An XML fragment is an XML instance that has a missing single top-level element. You can create columns and variables of the **XML** type and store XML instances in them. The **XML** data type and associated methods help integrate XML into the relational framework of SQL Server.

What is XPath?

XPath uses a set of expressions to select nodes to be processed. The most common expression that you'll use is the location path expression, which returns a set of nodes called a *node-set*. XPath can use both an unabbreviated an abbreviated syntax. The following is the unabbreviated syntax for a location path:

```
/axisName::nodeTest[predicate]/axisName::nodeTest[predicate]
```

What is Typed XML?

We can create variables, parameters, and columns of the XML type - if we associate a collection of XML schemas with a variable, parameter, or column of XML type. In this case, the XML data type instance is called typed XML. The fundamental advantage of using Typed XML is we can perform some amount of Validation constraints and even perform datatype validations.

How to Find Tables without Indexes?

Run the following query in the Query Editor.

```
USE <database_name>;
GO
SELECT SCHEMA_NAME(schema_id) AS schema_name
   ,name AS table_name
FROM sys.tables
WHERE OBJECTPROPERTY(OBJECT_ID,'IsIndexed') = 0
ORDER BY schema_name, table_name;
GO
```

How to find the Index Size of a Table?

We can use the following query to find the size of the index.

```
EXEC sp_spaceused [HumanResources.Shift]
```

How to Copy Data from One Table to Another Table?

There are multiple ways to do this.

1) INSERT INTO SELECT

This method is used when a table is already created in the database earlier and data have to be inserted into this table from another table. If columns listed in the INSERT clause and SELECT clause are the same, listing them is not required.

2) SELECT INTO

This method is used when a table is not created earlier and it needs to be created when data from one table must be inserted into a newly created table from another table. The new table is created using the same data types as those in the selected columns.

What are some of the limitations of the SELECT...INTO Clause?

We would highly recommend using INSERT...INTO...SELECT to copy data to another table. Some of the limitations for SELECT...INTO syntax are –

- You cannot specify a table variable or table-valued parameter as the new table.
- The FILESTREAM attribute does not transfer to the new table.
- Creates a new table in the default filegroup. SELECT...INTO does not use the partition scheme of the source table.
- Indexes, constraints, and triggers defined in the source table are not transferred to the new table
- When a computed column is included in the select list, the corresponding column in the new table is not a computed column
- User requires CREATE TABLE permission.

What is a Filestream?

Filestream allows you to store unstructured large objects (text documents, images, and videos) in the file system and have these files integrated within the database. FILESTREAM integrates the SQL Server Database Engine with New Technology File System (NTFS); it stores the data in varbinary (max) data type. Using this data type, the unstructured data is stored in the NTFS file system, and the SQL Server Database Engine manages the link between the Filestream column and the actual file located in the NTFS. Using Transact-SQL statements users can insert, update, delete and select the data stored in FILESTREAM-enabled tables.

What are some of the caveats working with Filestream data type?

Here are some of the interesting considerations with Filestream data type-

- The sizes of the BLOBs are limited only by the volume size of the NTFS file system.
- FILESTREAM data must be stored in FILESTREAM filegroups.
- FILESTREAM filegroups can be on compressed volumes.
- We can use all backup and recovery models with FILESTREAM data, and the FILESTREAM data is backed up with the structured data
- When using failover clustering, the FILESTREAM filegroups must be on shared disk resources.
- Encryption is not supported on FILESTREAM data.
- SQL Server does not support database snapshots for FILESTREAM filegroups.
- Database mirroring does not support FILESTREAM. While Log shipping and Replication support FILESTREAM datatypes.

What do you mean by TABLESAMPLE?

TABLESAMPLE allows you to extract a sampling of rows from a table in the FROM clause. The rows retrieved are random and they are not in any order. This sampling can be based on a percentage of several rows. You can use TABLESAMPLE when only a sampling of rows is necessary for the application instead of a full result set.

What are Ranking Functions?

Ranking functions return a ranking value for each row in a partition. All the ranking functions are non-deterministic. The different Ranking functions are as follows:

ROW_NUMBER () OVER ([<partition_by_clause>] <order_by_clause>)
Returns the sequential number of a row within a partition of a result set, starting at 1 for the first row in each partition.

RANK () OVER ([<partition_by_clause>] <order_by_clause>)
Returns the rank of each row within the partition of a result set.

DENSE_RANK () OVER ([<partition_by_clause>] <order_by_clause>)
Returns the rank of rows within the partition of a result set, without any gaps in the ranking.

NTILE (integer_expression) OVER ([<partition_by_clause>] <order_by_clause>)
Distributes the rows in an ordered partition into a specified number of groups.

What is ROW_NUMBER()?

ROW_NUMBER() returns a column as an expression that contains the row's number within the result set. This is only a number used in the context of the result set; if the result changes, the ROW_NUMBER() will change.

What is a ROLLUP Clause?

ROLLUP clause is used to do aggregate operation on multiple levels in a hierarchy. If we want to sum on different levels without adding any new column, then we can do it easily using ROLLUP. We have to just add the WITH ROLLUP Clause in the group by clause.

What is Change Data Capture (CDC) in SQL Server 2008?

Change Data Capture (CDC) records INSERTs, UPDATEs, and DELETEs applied to SQL Server tables and makes a record available of what changed, where, and when, in simple relational 'change tables' rather than in an esoteric chopped salad of XML. These change tables contain columns that reflect the column structure of the source table you have chosen to track along with the metadata needed to understand the changes that have been made.

How can I Track the Changes or Identify the Latest Insert-Update-Delete from a Table?

In SQL Server 2005 and earlier versions, there is no inbuilt functionality to know which row was recently changed and what the changes were. However, in SQL Server 2008, a new feature known as Change Data Capture (CDC) has been introduced to capture the changed data.

What is Change Tracking inside SQL Server?

Change tracking in SQL Server 2008 enables applications to obtain only changes that have been made to the user tables, along with the information about those changes. With change tracking integrated into SQL Server, complicated custom change tracking solutions no longer have to be developed.

What is Change Data Capture inside SQL Server?

Change data capture is designed to capture insert, update, and delete activity applied to SQL Server tables, and to make the details of the changes available in an easily consumed relational format. The change tables used by change data capture contain columns that mirror the column structure of a tracked source table, along with the metadata needed to understand the changes that have occurred.

How is Change Tracking is different from Change Data Capture?

The tracking mechanism in change data capture involves an asynchronous capture of changes from the transaction log so that changes are available after the DML operation. In change tracking, the tracking mechanism involves synchronous tracking of changes in line with DML operations so that change information is available immediately. In Change Data Capture Historical Data is tracked and in Change Tracking Historical Data is not tracked.

What is Auditing inside SQL Server?

SQL Server Audit offers features that help DBAs achieve their goals of meeting regulatory compliance requirements. SQL Server Audit provides centralized storage of audit logs and integration with System Center. SQL Server Audit was designed with the following primary goals in mind:

- Security – The audit feature, and its objects, must be truly secure.
- Performance - Performance impact must be minimized.
- Management – The audit feature must be easy to manage.
- Discoverability - Audit-centric questions must be easy to answer.

How is Auditing different from Change Data Capture?

CDC was created to help ETL scenarios by providing support for incremental data load. It uses an asynchronous capture mechanism that reads the transaction log and populates change capture tables with the row data and provides API's that provide access to that captured data in several ways. CDC is not to be used for auditing purposes.

Use SQL Server Auditing is a compliance need.

- Audits cannot / must not have an option to altered by any mechanism.
- CDC can be purged based on the retention period.
- SQL Server Audits can also keep track of SELECT statements
- Audits can also track Server changes (Login failures, DBCC commands execution etc) can also be tracked

These are some of the basic differences of CDC over SQL Server Audits.

How to get data from a Database on Another Server?

If you want to import data only through a T-SQL query, then use the OPENDATASOURCE function. To repeatedly get data from another server, create a linked server and then use the OPENQUERY function or use 4-part naming. If you do not adhere to T-SQL, then it is better to use the import/export wizard, and you can save it as an SSIS package for future use.

What is the Bookmark Lookup and RID Lookup?

When a small number of rows are requested by a query, the SQL Server optimizer will try to use a non-clustered index on the column or columns contained in the WHERE clause to retrieve the data requested by the query. If the query requests data from columns not present in the non-clustered index, then the SQL Server must go back to the data pages to get the data in those columns.

In the above scenario, if a table has clustered index, it is called **bookmark lookup** (or key lookup); if the table does not have clustered index, but in a heap, it is called **RID lookup**.

What is the difference between GETDATE and SYSDATETIME in SQL Server 2008?

In the case of GETDATE, the precision is till milliseconds, and in the case of SYSDATETIME, the precision is till 100th of a nanosecond.

What is the difference between GETUTCDATE and SYSUTCDATETIME functions?

These functions return data as UTC (Coordinated Universal Time). In the case of GETUTCDATE, the precision is till milliseconds. SYSUTCDATETIME has a default precision of 7 digits.

How to check if Automatic Statistic Update is Enabled for a database?

The following query can be used to know if Automatic Statistic Update:

```
SELECT is_auto_create_stats_on,is_auto_update_stats_on
FROM sys.databases
WHERE name ='YOUR DATABASE NAME HERE'
```

What is the Difference between Seek Predicate and Predicate?

Seek Predicate is the operation that describes the b-tree portion of the Seek. The predicate is the operation that describes the additional filter using non-key columns.

Based on the description, it is very clear that Seek Predicate is better than Predicate as it searches indexes, whereas, in Predicate, the search is on non-key a column – which implies that the search is on the data in a page, files itself.

What are the various Limitations of the Views?

- ORDER BY clause does not work in View.
- Regular queries or Stored Procedures give us flexibility when we need another column; we can add a column to regular queries right away. If we want to do the same with Views, then we will have to modify the first.
- Index created on view not used often.
- Once the view is created and if the basic table has any column added or removed, it is not usually reflected in the view till it is refreshed.
- One of the most prominent limitations of the View is that it does not support COUNT (*); however, it can support COUNT_BIG (*).

What are the Limitations of Indexed Views?

Some of the limitations with Indexed views are -

- UNION Operation is now allowed in Indexed View.
- We cannot create an Index on a nested View situation means we cannot create an index on a view that is built from another view.
- SELF JOIN Not Allowed in Indexed View.
- Outer Join Not Allowed in Indexed Views.
- Cross Database Queries Not Allowed in Indexed View.
- The view must be created WITH SCHEMABINDING option.
- ANSI_NULLS needs to be set for all existing tables that will be referenced in the view.
- Indexed Views cannot contain text, ntext, image, filestream, or XML columns.

What is a Covered index?

It is an index that can satisfy a query just by its index keys without having needed to touch the data pages is called Covering Index. It means that when a query is fired, SQL Server doesn't need to go to the table to retrieve the rows, but can produce the results directly from the index as the index covers all the columns used in a query.

When I Delete any Data from a Table, does the SQL Server reduce the size of that table?

When data are deleted from any table, the SQL Server does not reduce the size of the table right away; however, it marks those pages as free pages, showing that they belong to the table. When new data are inserted, they are put into those pages first. Once those pages are filled up, SQL Server will allocate new pages. If you wait for some time, the background process de-allocates the pages, finally reducing the page size.

Section 6: DBA Skills related Questions

How to Rebuild the Master Database?

Master database is a system database and it contains information about running server's configuration. When SQL Server 2005 is installed, it usually creates master, model, msdb, tempdb, resourcedb and the distribution system database by default. Only the Master database is the one that is absolutely a must-have database. Without the Master database, the SQL Server cannot be started. This is the reason why it is extremely important to back up the Master database.

To rebuild the Master database, run Setup.exe, verify, and repair a SQL Server instance, and rebuild the system databases. This procedure is most often used to rebuild the master database for a corrupted installation of SQL Server.

What are Standby Servers? Explain Types of Standby Servers.

A standby server is a type of server that can be brought online in a situation when the Primary Server goes offline and the application needs continuous (high) availability of the server. There is always a need to set up a mechanism where data and objects from the primary server are moved to a secondary (standby) server. This mechanism usually involves the process of moving back up from the primary server to the secondary server using T-SQL scripts. Often, database wizards are used to setting up this process.

Different types of standby servers are given as follows:

1) Hot Standby:

   Hot Standby can be achieved in the SQL Server using SQL Server 2005 Enterprise Edition and the later enterprise versions. SQL Server 2005 has introduced Mirroring of a database that can be configured for automatic failover in a disaster situation. In the case of synchronous mirroring, the database is replicated to both the servers simultaneously. This is a little expensive but provides the best high availability. In this case, both primary and standby servers have the same data all the time.

2) Warm Standby:

   In Warm Standby, automatic failover is not configured. This is usually set up using Log Shipping or asynchronous mirroring. Sometimes warm standby is lagging by a few minutes or seconds, which results in the loss of a few latest updates when the primary server fails and the secondary server needs to come online. Sometimes a warm standby server that is lagging by a few transactions is brought back to the current state by applying the recent transaction log.

3) Cold Standby:

   Code Standby servers need to be switched manually, and sometimes all the backups, as well as the required OS, need to be applied. Cold Standby just physically replaces the previous server.

What is the Difference between GRANT and WITH GRANT while Giving Permissions to the User?

In the case of the only GRANT, the username cannot grant the same permission to other users. On the other hand, with the option WITH GRANT, the username will be able to permit receiving requests from other users.

How to Copy the Tables, Schema and Views from one SQL Server to Another?

There are multiple ways to do this -

1) "Detach Database" from one server and "Attach Database" to another server.
2) Manually script all the objects using SSMS and run the script on a new server.
3) Use Wizard of SSMS.

Where are SQL server Usernames and Passwords Stored in the SQL server?

System Catalog Views, sys.server_principals and sys.sql_logins can show the various users in the system and these are stored in the master database.

What is SQLCMD?

sqlcmd is an enhanced version of the isql and osql, and it provides way more functionality than the other two options. In other words, sqlcmd is a better replacement of isql (which will be deprecated eventually) and osql (not included in SQL Server 2005 RTM). sqlcmd can work in two modes - i) BATCH and ii) interactive modes.

What is Utility Control Point (UCP)?

The SQL Server Utility models an organization's SQL Server-related entities in a unified view. Utility Explorer and SQL Server Utility viewpoints in (SSMS) provide administrators with a holistic view of resource health through an instance of SQL Server that serves as a utility control point (UCP). The UCP collects configuration and performance information from managed instances of SQL Server every 15 minutes by default.

What can be monitored via UCP?

Entities that can be viewed in the SQL Server UCP include:

- Instances of SQL Server
- Data-tier applications
- Database files
- Storage volumes

Resource utilization dimensions that can be viewed in the SQL Server UCP include:

- CPU utilization
- Storage space utilization

Some of the current restrictions include:

- The instance has to be SQL Server Relational Engine.
- Must be SQL 2008 R2 or SQL 2008 SP2 instance
- UCP cannot be done for Express editions
- Must operate within a single Windows domain, or across domains with two-way trust relationships.

How is sqlcmd different from osql?

SQLCMD utility is a command prompt utility to run ad-hoc T-SQL statements and scripts. You can also run sqlcmd interactively. SQLCMD is your new choice for scripting with SQL Server. There are interesting extended options that make SQLCMD worth using – like using the –A for DAC connections.

What is Data Collector?

SQL Server 2008 introduced the concept of data collector - you can obtain and save data that is gathered from several sources about SQL Server health. The data collector provides data collection containers that you can use to determine the scope and frequency of data collection on a SQL Server system. The data collector provides predefined collector types that you can use for data collection. The out-of-box collector types are –

- Generic T-SQL Query Collector Type
- Generic SQL Trace Collector Type
- Performance Counters Collector Type
- Query Activity Collector Type

What are the System Data Collection Sets predefined inside SQL Server?

During the installation, there are 3 System Data Collection are made available to DBAs. These to be later configured to monitor SQL Server. These cannot be deleted.

- **Disk Usage**: Collects data about disk and log usage for all the databases installed on the system.
- **Server Activity**: Collects resource usage statistics and performance data from the server and SQL Server.
- **Query Statistics**: Collects query statistics, individual query text, query plans, and specific queries.

When will you use SQLDiag tool?

The SQLdiag utility is a general-purpose diagnostics collection utility that can be run as a console application or as a service and can be very useful for Performance tuning exercises. SQLdiag is fully configurable through the SQLdiag.xml configuration file and can collect a variety of diagnostic information like Windows performance logs, Windows event logs, SQL Server Profiler traces, SQL Server blocking information and SQL Server configuration information.

What is the use of Dedicated Admin Connection (DAC)?

Dedicated Admin Connection allows user to connect to SQL server when normal connection attempts fail, for example, when a server is hanging, out of memory or other bad states that it's not responding to connection requests. DAC is achieved by pre-allocating dedicated resources during server startup, including memory and scheduler etc.

How to invoke a DAC Connection?

There are two fundamental way of connecting to DAC –

- You can use the sqlcmd which is the command prompt version and the osql version in SQL Server 2005. We have a new option **-A** that enables the connection to be as Admin connection.
- To enable the admin connection from SSMS you need to use the **ADMIN:** before your server's name

When would you use Server-side trace?

Running Profiler in a production environment is not a recommended practice on any day. To minimize this overhead server-side tracing via SQL Trace system stored procedures can be used but must be also with care.

What is the SP's used for creating, starting and stopping a Server-side trace?

The following are the system SPs that we can use to work with Server side trace -

- sp_trace_create - Creates a trace definition
- sp_trace_setevent - Alters an event or event column to a trace
- sp_trace_setfilter - Applies a filter to a trace
- sp_trace_setstatus - Starts, stop and close traces
- sp_trace_generateevent - Creates a user-defined event

What are the events on default trace?

The default SQL Server trace from SQL Server 2005 onwards is a background trace that runs continuously and records event information that can be useful in troubleshooting problems. Though the list is long, the following are captured by default trace –

- Data file auto grow
- Data file auto shrink
- Database mirroring status change
- Logfile auto grow
- Logfile auto shrink
- Error log
- Missing Column Statistics
- Missing Join Predicate
- Object Altered
- Object Created
- Object Deleted
- Server Memory Change

Apart from these many other SQL Server Security Auditing events are also captured like Add DB user event, DBCC event, Login Failed, Backup/Restore event, Server Starts and Stops and many more.

What is Central Management inside SQL Server?

SQL Server 2008 introduced a new method of administering multiple servers by enabling you to designate a Central Management Server. An instance of SQL Server that is designated as a Central Management Server maintains a list of registered servers. A typical usage for a DBA is to write a single query across servers to know the Version post a patch update across servers.

What tools are available for Extended Events?

For the SQL Server Engine, XEvent is configured using a series of T-SQL statements. There is no graphical tool support for XEvent in the current version of SQL Server 2008 R2. There are no tools provided that allow you to view the results of XEvent targets except those provided by Windows to view ETW data.

How to Enable/Disable Indexes?

```
--Disable Index
ALTERINDEX [IndexName] ON TableName DISABLE
GO

--Enable Index
ALTERINDEX [IndexName] ON TableName REBUILD
GO
```

What is Data Compression?

In SQL Server, Data Compression comes in many flavours:

- Row Compression
- Page Compression
- Dictionary Compression

Row Compression

Row compression changes the format of the physical storage of data. It minimizes the metadata (column information, length, offsets etc) associated with each record. Numeric data types and fixed-length strings are stored in variable-length storage format, just like Varchar.

Page Compression

Page compression allows common data to be shared between rows for a given page. It uses the following techniques to compress data:

- Row compression.
- Prefix Compression. For every column in a page, duplicate prefixes are identified. These prefixes are saved in compression information headers which resides after the page header. A reference number is assigned to these prefixes and that reference number is replaced where ever those prefixes are being used.

Dictionary Compression

Dictionary compression searches for duplicate values throughout the page and stores them in CI. The main difference between prefix and dictionary compression is that the former is only restricted to one column while the latter applies to the complete page.

What are Wait Types?

There are three types of wait types, namely,

Resource Waits. Resource waits occur when a worker requests access to a resource that is not available because that resource is either currently used by another worker or it's not yet available.

Queue Waits. Queue waits occur when a worker is idle, waiting for work to be assigned.

External Waits. External waits occur when an SQL Server worker is waiting for an external event.

What is 'FILLFACTOR'?

A "FILLFACTOR" is one of the important arguments that can be used while creating an index.

According to MSDN, FILLFACTOR specifies a percentage that indicates how much the Database Engine should fill each index page during index creation or rebuild. Fill-factor is always an integer-valued from 1 to 100. The fill-factor option is designed for improving index performance and data storage. By setting the fill-factor value, you specify the percentage of space on each page to be filled with data, reserving free space on each page for future table growth.

Specifying a fill-factor value of 70 would imply that 30 per cent of each page will be left empty, providing space for index expansion as data is added to the underlying table. Space is reserved between the index rows rather than at the end of the index. The fill-factor setting applies only when the index is created or rebuilt.

What are Points to Remember while Using the FILLFACTOR Argument?

- If the fill-factor is set to 100 or 0, the Database Engine fills pages to their capacity while creating indexes.
- The server-wide default FILLFACTOR is set to 0.
- To modify the server-wide default value, use the sp_configure system stored procedure.
- To view the fill-factor value of one or more indexes, use sys.indexes.
- To modify or set the fill-factor value for individual indexes, use CREATE INDEX or ALTER INDEX statements.
- Creating a clustered index with a FILLFACTOR < 100 may significantly increase the amount of space the data occupies because the Database Engine physically reallocates the data while building the clustered index.

Where in MS SQL Server '100' and '0' are equal?

Fill-factor settings of 0 and 100 are equal!

What is PAD_INDEX?

PAD_INDEX is the percentage of free space applied to the intermediate-level pages of the index as specified by the fill factor. The PAD_INDEX option is useful only when FILLFACTOR is specified.

What is the difference between a View and a Materialized View?

A ***view*** takes the output of a query and makes it appear like a virtual table, and it can be used in place of tables.
A ***materialized view*** provides indirect access to table data by storing the results of a query in a separate schema object.

What is the concept 'Optimize for ad hoc workloads' Option?

In SQL Server 2008, the "optimize for ad hoc workloads" option is a new server configuration option used to improve the efficiency of the plan cache for workloads that contain many single use ad hoc batches. This option is greatly useful for third party applications that the DBA might not have control over – like ERP, CRM systems are typical here.
When this option is set to 1, the Database Engine stores a small compiled plan stub in the plan cache when a batch is compiled for the first time, instead of the full compiled plan. This helps to relieve memory pressure by not allowing the plan cache to become filled with compiled plans that are not reused.

What is Policy Management?

Policy Management in SQL SERVER 2008 allows you to define and enforce policies for configuring and managing SQL Server across the enterprise. Policy-Based Management is configured in SQL Server Management Studio (SSMS). Navigate to the Object Explorer and expand the Management node and the Policy Management node; you will see the Policies, Conditions, and Facets nodes.

What are the Basics of Policy Management?

SQL server 2008 has introduced a policy management framework, which is the latest technique for SQL server database engine. SQL policy administrator uses SQL Server Management Studio to create policies that can handle entities on the server side like the SQL Server objects and the instance of SQL Server databases. It consists of three components: policy administrators (who create policies), policy management, and explicit administration. Policy-based management in SQL Server assists the database administrators in defining and enforcing policies that tie to database objects and instances. These policies allow the administrator to configure and manage SQL server across the enterprise.

What are the Policy Management Terms?

To have a better grip on the concept of Policy-based management, there are some key terms you need to understand.

Target – A type of entity that is appropriately managed by Policy-based management. For example, a table, database and index, to name a few.

Facet -A property that can be managed in policy-based management. A clear example of a facet is the name of a Trigger or the Auto Shrink property of the database.

Conditions – Criteria that specifies the state of facet to true or false. For example, you can adjust the state of a facet that gives you clear specifications of all stored procedures in the Schema 'Banking'.

Policy – A set of rules specified for the server objects or the properties of the database.

What are the Advantages of Policy Management?

The following advantages can be achieved by appropriate administration of the policy management system.

- It interacts with various policies for successful system configuration.
- It handles the changes in the systems that are the result of configuration against authoring policies.
- It reduces the cost of ownership with a simple elaboration of administration tasks.
- It detects various compliance issues in SQL Server Management Studio.

What is Transparent Data Encryption?

Transparent data encryption (TDE) introduces a new database option that encrypts the database files automatically, without needing to alter any applications. This prevents unauthorized users from accessing a database, even if they obtain the database files or database backup files.

Transparent data encryption (TDE) performs real-time I/O encryption and decryption of the data and log files. The encryption uses a database encryption key (DEK), which is stored in the database boot record for availability during recovery.

What is "Extensible Key Management" in SQL Server?

The extensible key management (EKM) feature allows third-party enterprise key management and hardware security module (HSM) vendors to register their devices in SQL Server. Once registered, SQL Server users can use the encryption keys stored on these modules, as well as leveraging the advanced encryption features that these modules support, such as bulk encryption/decryption and many key management functions such as key ageing and key rotation. Data can be encrypted and decrypted using TSQL cryptographic statements, and SQL Server uses the external EKM device as the key store.

What are Signed Modules?

SQL Server 2005 introduced the capability to sign modules within the database, such as stored procedures, functions, triggers or assemblies. The need to encrypt the definition of the logic inside these procedures and function has been there for ages for enterprises. Signed Modules are an efficient and powerful way to do the same. By signing a Module with a certificate, the certificate is then granted the relevant permission and goes beyond what can be achieved with the "Execute As" feature, especially from an auditing perspective.

What is the Use of DBCC Commands?

The Transact-SQL programming language provides DBCC statements that act as Database Console Commands for SQL Server. DBCC commands are used to perform the following tasks.

- Maintenance tasks on database, index, or filegroup.
- Tasks that gather and display various types of information.
- Validation operations on a database, table, index, catalog, filegroup, or allocation of database pages.
- Miscellaneous tasks such as enabling trace flags or removing a DLL from memory.

What is the difference between ROLLBACK IMMEDIATE and WITH NO_WAIT during ALTER DATABASE?

ROLLBACK AFTER integer [SECONDS] | ROLLBACK IMMEDIATE:

Specifies whether to roll back after a specified number of seconds or immediately if a transaction is not complete.

NO_WAIT:

Specifies that if the requested database state or option change cannot complete immediately without waiting for transactions to commit or rollback on their own, then the request will fail.

What are Replication and Database Mirroring?

Database mirroring can be used with replication to provide availability for the publication database. Database mirroring involves two copies of a single database that typically reside on different computers. At any given time, only one copy of the database is currently available to clients, which is known as the principal database. Updates made by the clients to the principal database are applied to the other copy of the database, known as the mirror database. Mirroring involves applying the transaction log from every insertion, update, or deletion made on the principal database onto the mirror database.

What is the Database Mirroring enhancements done with SQL Server 2008 R2?

There were some enhancements done with DBM, some to call out are -

- Write-ahead on the incoming log stream on the mirror server.
- Improved use of log send buffers.
- Compression of the stream of transaction log records.
- Automatic Recovery from Corrupted Pages

What is a peer to peer replication?

Peer-to-peer replication is a special type of Transactional replication extension that provides a scale-out and high-availability solution by maintaining copies of data across multiple server instances. Peer-to-peer replication propagates transactionally consistent changes in near real-time. To avoid potential data inconsistency, make sure that you avoid conflicts in a peer-to-peer topology, even with conflict detection enabled.

What is bidirectional transactional Replication

Bidirectional transactional replication is a specific form of transactional replication that allows both the Publisher and the Subscriber to send data to each other. The better option here would be to use peer-to-peer replication.

What is Failover clustering?

With failover clustering, the nodes share disks, but only a single node has access to the database at a time. It is possible to install additional SQL Server failover cluster instances across the nodes; however, this configuration cannot be used to re-direct workloads for a single database (for example, separating reads from writes).

What are the questions and considerations you will make for HA/DR design?

- Understand prioritized HA/DR requirements for the application. What is the SLA's set by the customer?
- Are customers comfortable or budgeted for a shared storage solution?
- What is the recovery point objective (RPO)? This decides the combination of configurations like - Failover clustering is often deployed alongside database mirroring, with clustering used for local HA, and database mirroring used for DR.
- Consider a Geo cluster (or stretch cluster) as a combined HA/DR solution. This solution requires software to enable the cluster and storage-level replication and from the storage vendor
- What is the recovery time objective (RTO)? How fast the system has to get online after say a site failure.

Though these are some of the high-level questions, these do help narrow down to a solution quickly or at least to a couple of options.

What is the concept of Piecemeal restore on SQL Server?

Online PIECEMEAL RESTORE is available from SQL Server 2005 Enterprise Edition, this allows administrators of databases that employ multiple filegroups to restore missing filegroups in stages while the database is online.

What are OFFLINE datafiles with SQL Server?

The OFFLINE directive is a new feature of the ALTER DATABASE command. This allows databases that employ multiple filegroups to be online serving queries, while some of the database data may unavailable, in one or more filegroup(s) marked as offline.

Why can't I run TRUNCATE TABLE on a published table?

TRUNCATE TABLE is a minimally-logged operation and it does not fire any triggers. It is not possible to use them on replicated databases because replication cannot track the changes caused by the operation: transactional replication tracks changes through the transaction log; merge replication tracks changes through triggers on published tables.

If any Stored Procedure is Encrypted, then can we see its definition in Activity Monitor?

No, we can’t see the definition of encrypted stored procedure in Activity Monitor.

What are the different states a Database can get into?

The standard states as defined in sys.databases are -
0 = ONLINE
1 = RESTORING
2 = RECOVERING
3 = RECOVERY_PENDING
4 = SUSPECT
5 = EMERGENCY
6 = OFFLINE

How to Stop Log File Growing too Big?

If your Transaction Log file was growing too big and you wanted to manage its size, then instead of truncating the transaction log file,
you should choose one of the options mentioned below.

1) Convert the Recovery Model to Simple Recovery
   If you change your recovery model to the Simple Recovery Model, then you will not encounter the extraordinary growth of your log file.
2) Start Taking Transaction Log Backup
   In this Full Recovery Model, your transaction log will grow until you take a backup of it. You need to take the T-Log Backup at a regular interval. This way, your log would not grow beyond some limits.

What is Resource Governor in SQL Server?

The Resource Governor is a feature given by SQL Server 2008 to control and allocate CPU and memory resources depending on the priority of applications. Resource Governor will control the allocation of CPU, Memory for the SQL Server Relational Engine Instance.

How would you define a Resource Governor?

There a 3 core fundamental concepts required to define a Resource Governor are –

- Resource Pools – These define the various groups of resources that can be used within the server. You can define groups for CPU and Memory buckets into which workloads are defined.
- Workload Groups - A workload group serves as a container for session requests so that there can be predictable performance guaranteed for the group. Typical classification can be CxO group, reporting group, Developer group, Admin Group etc.
- Classification Function – this is based on a set of user-written criteria (UDF) contained in a function. The results of the function logic enable Resource Governor to classify sessions into existing workload groups.

How to restart SQL Server in single-user mode?

There are a couple of ways to start SQL Server in single-user mode –

- You can start an instance of SQL Server in single-user mode by using the startup option –m
- You can use -m option with sqlcmd or Management Studio
- You can also start sqlservr.exe with –m option

What are the different backup options with SQL Server?

At the high-level, there are 3 most important backups to understand –

- **Full Backup** – these backups contain ALL the data in a specific database.
- **Differential backup** - A differential backup contains only the data that has changed since the differential base. At restore time, the full backup is restored first, followed by the most recent differential backup.
- **Transactional Log Backups** - The transaction log is a serial record of all the transactions that have been performed against the database since the transaction log was last backed up. With transaction log backups, you can recover the database to a specific point in time or the point of failure in the FULL recovery model.

There are other special types of backups that we didn't cover include –

- Partial Backup
- File Backup
- Differential Partial Backup
- Differential File Backup
- Copy-Only Backups

What are the different recovery models inside SQL Server?

There are 3 different recovery models inside SQL Server-

- **Simple Recovery model** – with minimum administrative overhead for the transaction log, the simple recovery model risks significant work-loss exposure if the database is damaged. Data is recoverable only to the most recent backup.
- **Bulk-Logged recovery model** – Used for bulk operations, for large-scale such as bulk import or index creation, switching temporarily to the bulk-logged recovery model increases performance and reduces log space consumption. Log backups are still required.

- **Full Recovery Model** - The full recovery model guarantees the least risk of losing work if a data file is damaged. In this model, SQL Server fully logs all operations. In this recovery model, you can recover to a Point-in-time and is the most recommended model for financially systems.

What is the difference between DB Mirroring and Log Shipping?

Log Shipping is one of the oldest forms of High-Availability Strategy inside SQL Server. The concept here is the primary database on the server is backed up and restored on one or more servers as secondary's. After this step, transaction logs are restored from the primary onto the secondary over a periodic interval defined.

Database mirroring provides a redundant copy of a single database that is automatically configured to update the changes. Database mirroring works by sending transaction log records from the main principal database to the mirror server. The transaction log records are then replayed on the mirror database continuously. Some of the differences include -

- A log shipping secondary can also be set to allow read-only access to the database in between transaction log restore operations.
- The log shipping process is controlled through SQL Server Agent jobs that perform the backups, copies, restores and monitoring.
- Database Mirroring can detect failures automatically. Even automatic page repairs are possible.
- With Database Mirroring failovers can also be automated.

What are the Plan Guides?

From SQL Server 2005, there is a new feature called Plan Guides that can help out in cases where you discover poorly performing queries that you don't have direct control over like ones made by third-party applications. Plan guides influence the optimization of queries by attaching query hints to them. When the query executes, SQL Server matches the query to the plan guide and attaches the OPTION clause to the query at run time.

How can you validate a backup copy of your database?

The best option to validate a backup copy is the RESTORE VERIFYONLY command. This option checks to see that the backup set is complete and the entire backup is readable. However, RESTORE VERIFYONLY does not attempt to verify the structure of the data contained in the backup volumes.

What is an ONLINE rebuilding of Indexes?

Online operation means when online operations are happening the database is in normal operational condition, the processes which are participating in online operations does not require exclusive access to a database. In the case of Online Indexing Operations, when Index operations (create, rebuild, dropping) are occurring they do not require exclusive access to a database, they do not lock any database tables. This is a major important upgrade in SQL Server from previous versions.

What are the steps to create a table partition?

There are 3 steps for creating a table partition –

- Partition Function – This defines "how" you want to partition the data.
- Partition Scheme – This defines "where" each of the partition defined by the function resides.
- Attaching the Partition Scheme to Table – You map the Partition Scheme to the table based on a column's data using the ON clause in a table definition.

What are the various page verification options in SQL Server 2008?

Between the time SQL Server writes a page to disk, then later reads the same page, it is possible that the data stored in the page may get corrupted due to circumstances outside the control of SQL Server. While SQL Server cannot prevent corruption outside of its control, it does at least have the ability to identify corrupt data. In SQL Server 2005 and SQL Server 2008, you can choose from one of three PAGE_VERIFY options:

- NONE
- CHECKSUM
- TORN_PAGE_DETECTION

CHECKSUM works by calculating a checksum over the contents of the whole page and stores the value in the page header when a page is written to disk. When the page is read from the disk, the checksum is recomputed and compared to the checksum value stored in the page header. A checksum failure indicates an I/O path problem.

What are some of the operations that cannot be done on the Model Database?

Some of the restrictions when working with Model Database is-

- We cannot add files or filegroups
- The default collation is the server collation and cannot be changed.
- We cannot drop this database.
- Setting the database to OFFLINE is not available.
- Setting the database or primary filegroup to READ_ONLY is not allowed

How can Index fragmentation be removed inside SQL Server?

Some of the most common methods of removing fragmentation are using the following DDLs-

- CREATE INDEX...DROP EXISTING
- ALTER INDEX...REORGANIZE
- ALTER INDEX...REBUILD
- DROP INDEX; CREATE INDEX

How can you disable Indexes inside SQL Server?

As an administrator, Disabling Indexes feature which is available in SQL Server 2005 and later versions to prevent the index usage by user queries. When you are disabling an index the index definition remains in metadata and index statistics are also kept for non-clustered indexes. You can use the following command to disable an index –

```
ALTER INDEX IX_Address_StateProvinceID ON Person.Address DISABLE
```

To re-enable an index, the following command can be used or CREATE INDEX WITH DROP_EXISTING Statement can be used –

```
ALTER INDEX IX_Address_StateProvinceID ON Person.Address REBUILD
```

Section 7: Data Warehousing Interview Questions & Answers

What is Business Intelligence (BI)?

Business Intelligence (BI) refers to technologies, applications and practices for the collection, integration, analysis, and presentation of business information and sometimes to the information itself. The purpose of BI is to support better business decision making. Thus, BI is also described as a decision support system (DSS).

BI systems provide historical, current, and predictive views of business operations, most often using data that has been gathered into a data warehouse or a data mart and occasionally working from operational data.

What is Data Warehousing?

A data warehouse is the main repository of an organization's historical data, its corporate memory. It contains the raw material for management's decision support system. The critical factor leading to the use of a data warehouse is that a data analyst can perform complex queries and analysis, such as data mining, on the information without slowing down the operational systems (Ref: Wikipedia). Data warehousing collection of data designed to support management decision making. Data warehouses contain a wide variety of data that present a coherent picture of business conditions at a single point in time. It is a repository of integrated information, available for queries and analysis.

What are some characteristics of typical Data Warehousing?

- Subject-oriented, which means that the data in the database is organized so that all the data elements relating to the same real-world event or object are linked together;
- Time-variant, which means that the changes to the data in the database are tracked and recorded so that reports can be produced showing changes over time;
- Non-volatile, which means that data in the database is never over-written or deleted, once committed, the data is static, read-only, but retained for future reporting.
- Integrated, which means that the database contains data from most or all of an organization's operational applications and that this data is made consistent.

What languages used for BI workloads?

BI uses the following languages to achieve the Goal.

MDX – Multidimensional Expressions:

This language is used for retrieving data from SSAS cubes. It looks very similar to T-SQL, but it is very different in the areas of conceptualization and implementation.

DMX – Data Mining Extensions:

This is again used for SSAS, but rather than cubes it is used for data mining structures. This language is more complicated than MDX. Microsoft has provided many wizards in its BI tools, which further reduced the number of experts for learning this language, which deals with data mining structures.

XMLA – XML for Analysis:

This is mainly used for SSAS administrative tasks. It is quite commonly used in administration tasks such as backup or restore database, copy and move the database, or learning Metadata information. Again, MS BI tools provide a lot of wizards for the same.

DAX – Data Analysis Expressions:

The Data Analysis Expressions (DAX) language is a new formula language that you can use in PowerPivot workbooks. DAX is not a subset of MDX, but a new formula language that is considered an extension of the formula language in Excel.

What is a Dimension Table?

A dimensional table contains textual attributes of measurements stored in the facts tables. The dimensional table is a collection of hierarchies, categories and logic that can be used for the user to traverse in hierarchical nodes.

What is the Hierarchy?

Hierarchy is the specification of levels that represents the relationship between different attributes within a dimension. For example, one possible hierarchy in the Time dimension is Year → Quarter → Month → Day.

What is a Fact Table?

The fact table contains measurements of the business process. Fact table contains the foreign keys for the dimension tables. For instance, if your business process is 'paper production', 'average production of paper by one machine' or 'weekly production of paper' will be considered as the measurement of the business process.

What is a Level of Granularity of a Fact Table?

The level of granularity means the level of detail that you put into the fact table in a data warehouse. The level of granularity implies the detail you are willing to put for each transactional fact.

What is the Factless Facts Table?

A fact table that does not contain numeric fact columns is called a factless facts table.

What is a Conformed Fact?

Conformed dimensions are the dimensions that can be used across multiple Data Marts in combination with multiple facts tables accordingly.

What are Non-Additive Facts?

Non-additive facts are facts that cannot be summed up for any of the dimensions present in the fact table. However, they are not considered useless. If there are changes in dimensions, the same facts can be useful.

What are Aggregate tables?

Aggregate tables are used to store summaries of fact tables. These are typical methods used to improve performance and can also be used with OLTP workloads. OLAP cubes contain pre-aggregated tables based on the modeling.

What is Dimensional Modeling?

The Dimensional data model concept involves two types of tables and it is different from the 3rd normal form. This concept uses the *Facts* table, which contains the measurements of the business, and the *Dimension* table, which contains the context (dimension of calculation) of the measurements.

What are the Conformed Dimensions?

Conformed dimensions mean the same thing with every possible fact table to which they are joined. They are common to the cubes.

What are Slowly Changing Dimensions (SCD)?

SCD is the abbreviation of slowly changing dimensions. SCD applies to cases where the attribute for a record varies over time. There are three different types of SCD.

1) SCD1: The new record replaces the original record. Only one record exists in the database - current data.
2) SCD2: A new record is added to the customer dimension table. Two records exist in the database - current data and previous historical data.
3) SCD3: The original data is modified to include new data. One record exists in the database - new information is attached with old information in the same row.

What is Hybrid Slowly Changing Dimension?

Hybrid SCDs are a combination of both SCD 1 and SCD 2. It may happen that in a table, some columns are important and we need to track changes for them, i.e. capture the historical data for them, whereas in some columns even if the data changes, we do not care.

How do you Load the Time Dimension?

Time dimensions are usually loaded by a program that loops through all possible dates that may appear in the data. 100 years may be represented in a time dimension, with one row per day.

Why is Data Modeling Important?

Data modeling is probably the most labour intensive and time-consuming part of the development process. The goal of the data model is to make sure that all data objects required by the database are completely and accurately represented. Because the data model uses easily understood notations and natural language, it can be reviewed and verified as correct by the end-users.

In computer science, data modeling is the process of creating a data model by applying a data model theory to create a data model instance. A data model theory is a formal data model description. In data modeling, we are structuring and organizing data. These data structures are then typically implemented in a database management system. In addition to defining and organizing the data, data modeling will impose (implicitly or explicitly) constraints or limitations on the data placed within the structure.

Managing large quantities of structured and unstructured data is a primary function of information systems. Data models describe structured data for storage in data management systems such as relational databases. They typically do not describe unstructured data, such as word processing documents, email messages, pictures, digital audio, and video.

What are the Fundamental Stages of Data Warehousing?

There are four different stages of the Data Warehousing lifecycle –

Offline Operational Databases:

Data warehouses in this initial stage are developed by simply copying the database of an operational system to an off-line server where the processing load of reporting does not impact the operational system's performance.

Offline Data Warehouse:

Data warehouses in this stage of evolution are updated on a regular time cycle (usually daily, weekly or monthly) from the operational systems, and the data is stored in an integrated reporting-oriented data structure.

Real-Time Data Warehouse:

Data warehouses at this stage are updated on a transaction or event basis, every time an operational system performs a transaction (e.g. an order or a delivery or a booking).

Integrated Data Warehouse:

Data warehouses at this stage are used to generate activity or transactions that are passed back into the operational systems for use in the daily activity of the organization.

What are the Different Methods of Loading Dimension tables?

There are two different ways to load data in dimension tables.

Conventional (Slow):

All the constraints and keys are validated against the data before it is loaded; this way data integrity is maintained.

Direct (Fast):

All the constraints and keys are disabled before the data is loaded. Once data is loaded, it is validated against all the constraints and keys. If data is found invalid or dirty, it is not included in the index, and all future processes on this data are skipped.

Describes the Foreign Key Columns in the Fact Table and Dimension Table?

Foreign keys of dimension tables are the primary keys of entity tables. Foreign keys of facts tables are the primary keys of dimension tables.

What is Data Mining?

Data Mining is the process of analyzing data from different perspectives and summarizing it into useful information. Data Mining takes the analysis to the next stage by applying models on test data to get trends, hidden correlations of attributes and even build probability scenario for future data.

What is the Difference between OLTP and OLAP?

Data Source

OLTP: Operational data is from the original data source of the data

OLAP: Consolidation data is from various sources.

Process Goal

OLTP: Snapshot of business processes that do fundamental business tasks

OLAP: Multi-dimensional views of business activities of planning and decision making

Queries and Process Scripts

OLTP: Simple quick running queries ran by users.

OLAP: Complex long-running queries by the system to update the aggregated data.

Database Design

OLTP: Normalized small database. Speed will be not an issue because of a small database, and normalization will not degrade performance. This adopts the entity-relationship (ER) model and an application-oriented database design.

OLAP: De-normalized large database. Speed is an issue because of a large database and de-normalizing will improve performance as there will be fewer tables to scan while performing tasks. This adopts star, snowflake or fact constellation mode of subject-oriented database design.

Back up and System Administration

OLTP: Regular Database backup and system administration can do the job.

OLAP: Reloading the OLTP data is considered a good backup option.

What is the difference between OLAP and Data Warehouse?

Data Warehouse is the place where the data is stored for analysis, whereas OLAP is the process of analyzing the data, managing aggregations, partitioning information into cubes for in-depth visualization.

What is ODS?

ODS is the abbreviation of Operational Data Store - a database structure that is a repository for near real-time operational data rather than long-term trend data. The ODS may further become the enterprise-shared operational database, allowing operational systems that are being re-engineered to use the ODS as their operation databases.

What is ETL?

ETL is an abbreviation of extract, transform, and load. ETL is software that enables businesses to consolidate their disparate data while moving it from place to place, and it doesn't matter that that data is in different forms or formats. The data can come from any source. ETL is powerful enough to handle such data disparities. First, the extract function reads data from a specified source database and extracts a desired subset of data. Next, the transform function works with the acquired data - using rules or lookup tables, or creating combinations with other data - to convert it to the desired state. Finally, the load function is used to write the resulting data to a target database.

What is VLDB?

VLDB is an abbreviation of Very Large Database. For instance, a one-terabyte database can be considered as a VLDB. Typically, these are decision support systems or transaction processing applications serving a large number of users.

Is the OLTP Database is Design Optimal for Data Warehouse?

No. OLTP database tables are normalized, and it will add additional time to queries to return results. Additionally, the OLTP database is small; it does not contain data from a long period (many years), which needs to be analyzed. An OLTP system is an ER model and not a Dimensional Model. If a complex query is executed on an OLTP system, it may lead to heavy overhead on the OLTP server that will affect the normal business processes.

If denormalizing improves Data Warehouse Processes, then why is the Fact Table is in the Normal Form?

The foreign keys of facts tables are the primary keys of dimension tables. The fact table contains columns that are a primary key to another table that itself make a normal form table.

What are Lookup Tables?

A lookup table is a table placed on the target table based upon the primary key of the target; it just updates the table by allowing only modified (new or updated) records based on the lookup condition.

What is Real-Time Data-Warehousing?

Data warehousing captures business activity data. Real-time data warehousing captures business activity data as it occurs. As soon as the business activity is complete and there is data about it, the completed activity data flows into the data warehouse and becomes available instantly.

What is BUS Schema?

BUS Schema consists of a master suite of confirmed dimension and standardized definition of facts.

What is a Star Schema?

Star schema is a type of organizing the tables such that we can retrieve the result from the database quickly in the warehouse environment.

What Snow Flake Schema?

In Snowflake Schema, each dimension has a primary dimension table, to which one or more additional dimensions can join. The primary dimension table is the only table that can join the fact table.

Differences between the Star and Snowflake Schema?

Star schema: A single fact table with N number of dimensions; all dimensions will be linked directly with a fact table. This schema is de-normalized and results in simple join and less complex query as well as faster results.

Snow schema: Any dimension with extended dimensions is known as snowflake schema; dimensions may be interlinked or may have a one-to-many relationship with other tables. This schema is normalized and results in complex join leading to very complex query (as well as slower results).

What is the ER Diagram?

Entity-Relationship (ER) Diagrams are a major data modeling tool and will help organize the data in your project into entities and define the relationships between the entities. This process has enabled the analyst to produce a good database structure so that the data can be stored and retrieved most efficiently.

An entity-relationship (ER) diagram is a specialized graphic that illustrates the interrelationships between entities in a database. A type of diagram used in data modeling for relational databases. These diagrams show the structure of each table and the links between tables.

What is the difference between ER Modeling and Dimensional Modeling?

ER modeling is used for normalizing the OLTP database design. Dimensional modeling is used for de-normalizing the ROLAP/MOLAP design.

What is a Degenerate Dimension Table?

If a table contains values, which are neither dimension nor measures, then it is called a degenerate dimension table.

What is a Surrogate Key?

A surrogate key is a substitution for the natural primary key. It is just a unique identifier or number for each row that can be used for the primary key to the table. The only requirement for a surrogate primary key is that it should be unique for each row in the table. It is useful because the natural primary key can change and this makes updates more difficult. Surrogated keys are always integer or numeric.

What is Junk Dimension?

Several very small dimensions may get lumped together to form a single dimension, i.e. a junk dimension - the attributes are not closely related. Grouping Random flags and text Attributes in a dimension and moving them to a separate sub dimension is known as junk dimension.

What is a Data Mart?

A data mart (DM) is a specialized version of a data warehouse (DW). Like data warehouses, data marts contain a snapshot of operational data that helps business people to strategize based on analyses of past trends and experiences. The key difference is that the creation of a data mart is predicated on a specific, predefined need for a certain grouping and configuration of select data. A data mart configuration emphasizes easy access to relevant information (Reference: Wiki). Data Marts are designed to help the manager make strategic decisions about their business.

What is a Cube and Linked Cube regarding Data Warehouse?

Cubes are a logical representation of multidimensional data. The edge of the cube contains dimension members and the body of the cube contains data values. The linking in the cube ensures that the data in the cubes remain consistent.

What is Snapshot regarding Data Warehouse?

You can disconnect the report from the catalog to which it is attached by saving the report with a snapshot of the data.

What is MDS?

Master Data Services or MDS helps enterprises standardize the data people rely on to make critical business decisions. With Master Data Services, IT organizations can centrally manage critical data assets companywide and across diverse systems, enable more people to securely manage master data directly, and ensure the integrity of information over time.

Explain the Paradigm of Bill Inmon and Ralph Kimball.

Bill Inmon's paradigm: Data warehouse is one part of the overall business intelligence system. An enterprise has one data warehouse, and data marts source their information from the data warehouse. In the data warehouse, information is stored in the 3rd normal form.

Ralph Kimball's paradigm: Data warehouse is the conglomerate of all data marts within the enterprise. Information is always stored in the dimensional model.

What are the different kinds of report parameter?

Reporting services uses two different kinds of parameters -

Query Parameter:

- The query parameters are defined as part of the dataset query and processed on the database server.
- If the query contains a query parameter, Reporting Services automatically creates a report parameter based on the name of the query parameter. Query parameters are mapped to report parameters so that users or report authors can pass back the value to use in the query.

Report Parameter:

- A report parameter is a variable defined at the report level that allows the personalization of the report at the run time.
- Report parameters differ from query parameters in that they are defined in a report and processed by the report server.
- Each time you add a report parameter to the report, a new member is added to the Parameters collection for you to use in an expression.

What are the command line tools to execute SSIS packages?

DTSEXECUI – When this command-line tool is run a user interface is loaded to configure each of the applicable parameters to execute an SSIS package.
DTEXEC – This is a pure command-line tool where all of the needed switches must be passed into the command for the successful execution of the SSIS package.

What is a control flow inside SSIS?

In SQL Server Integration Services (SSIS) a workflow is called a control-flow. Control-flow links together our various data-flows as a series of operations to achieve the final result. A control flow consists of one or more tasks and containers that execute when the package runs.

What are the different control flow elements inside SSIS?

SSIS provides three different types of control flow elements: containers that provide structures in packages, tasks that provide functionality, and precedence constraints that connect the executables, containers, and tasks into an ordered control flow.

What is the data flow?

A data flow consists of the sources and destinations that extract and load data, the transformations that modify and transform data, and the paths that link sources, transformations and destinations.

What are the different components of the data flow?

SQL Server Integration Services (SSIS) provides three different types of data flow components: sources, transformations, and destinations.

- Sources extract data from data stores such as tables and views in relational databases, files, and Analysis Services databases.
- Transformations modify, summarize, and clean data.
- Destinations load data into data stores or create in-memory datasets.

Explain the different options for dynamic configurations with SSIS?

There are 4 different ways of storing and accessing configuration information from within SSIS -

- Use an XML config file
- Use custom environmental variables
- Use a database per environment with the variables
- Use a centralized database with all variables

What are the different Lookup Cache modes in SSIS?

There are 3 Cache Modes available in SSIS Lookup Transformation as follows:

- Full Cache Mode
- Partial Cache Mode
- No Cache Mode

Explain Partial Cache Mode?

In Partial Cache Mode, SSIS queries the database against new rows coming in from the source and if matched then that row is cached into SSIS Lookup Cache for rows coming subsequently in the data flow. When the cache becomes full, SSIS removes a few of the rows from the cache based on the usage/match statistics for those rows and loads the new matching rows into the Lookup Cache.

What is the use of SSIS Data profiler?

SQL Server 2008 introduced the new feature of Data Profiler with SSIS. Data Profiler helps you understand the number of distinct values in each column, distribution of data, Mean (average) and standard deviation of the data values, Minimum and maximum values of the data, Column length distribution, NULL Ratios, Column Patterns etc. This is highly recommended during performance tuning exercise to know your data sampling and Data Profiler is a great task to have. In performance testing, you might want to mimic data distribution as on production to a similar-sized distribution on the test environment for a particular columnar data.

What do you mean by Repeating Data Regions inside SSRS?

The concept of nested data regions to display the same data region multiple times in your report is called Repeating Data Regions. Datasets for both data regions must be the same. If you need to create a report that uses grouping like this (such as in a master-detail page) but with different datasets, use a sub-report.

What are the Differences between SSRS 2005 and SSRS 2008 versions?

Report Server 2008 is a complete architectural rewrite; from the report processing engine and the report renderers to the fact that it no longer depends on IIS to host the Report Server and Report Manager. The following areas could have major implications for support:

- Removal of IIS as a dependency
- On-Demand "Pull" model of report processing
- Consolidated renderer code
- New data visualization controls
- New Report Designer

Areas with minimal changes are:

- Report Builder
- SharePoint Integration
- Client Print Control
- Report Manager user interface
- Report Server web method APIs
- Command-line tools

What is PowerPivot?

PowerPivot is comprised of numerous different client and server components that provide customers with an end to end solution for creating business intelligence via the familiar interface of Microsoft Excel 2010.

PowerPivot for SharePoint adds server-side applications and features that support PowerPivot data access and management for workbooks that you publish to SharePoint. PowerPivot server components load the data, process queries, perform scheduled data refresh, and track server and workbook usage in the farm.

What is PowerPivot for Excel?

PowerPivot for Excel allows customers to create PowerPivot IMBI databases within the Excel process space. The data is stored in the actual workbook itself. The workbook contains the embedded data that is extracted and processed by the Vertipaq engine which is Analysis Services running in process inside of excel. There is no need to connect to a server to work with the data once downloaded.

What is Master Data?

Master data is slowly changing reference data shared across systems. This master data describes the critical "nouns" of the business that typically fall into the following categories: People, Things, Places or Abstract concepts.

Section 8: General Best Practices

Here are some quick notes on some generic best practices. These are sometimes subjective based on the situation but we consider these can still apply to most of the systems we work with. Don't take these words as written on stone but just a guiding content.

- **Do** de-normalize if necessary, for the performance
- **Do** define the Primary Key as clustered. This keeps the secondary indexes much smaller.
- **Do** create indexes on the Foreign Key columns.
- **Do** select the correct "Recovery Model" for a database.
- **Do** use 100% Fill Factor on read-only or seldom updated tables.
- **Do Not** over-index, make sure you know which indexes will be used.
- **Do Not** use special characters when creating database objects.
- **Do** use consistent abbreviations of similar words. If the Charge is CHRG then Change should be CHNG.
- **Do Not** use spaces or special characters in column names.
- iSCSI storage area networks is a viable solution where cost is an issue
- Use redundant, dedicated gigabit Ethernet NICs for iSCSI connectivity
- **Do not** enable network protocols unless they are needed
- **Do not** expose a server that is running SQL Server to the public Internet.
- Make sure the tables have statistics. Keeping Auto-generate stats and Auto create stats options on in the database is the default. For read-only databases, it may be necessary to manually create statistics.
- **No undocumented** system stored procedures should be employed.
- When calling a stored procedure with parameters, it's a good idea to name the parameter and the value instead of just supplying the values in order.
- **Avoid** altering the ANSI settings with SET in procedures, as doing so causes stored procedure recompiles
- Having datatype mismatches between columns that are in a primary/foreign key relationship or for parameter and values mismatch must be avoided.
- **Do not** implement security as an afterthought in the development process
- Use "allow only encrypted connections" only if needed for end-to-end encryption of sensitive sessions
- Grant CONNECT permission only on endpoints to logins that need to use them. Explicitly deny CONNECT permission to endpoints that are not needed by users or groups
- Install only those components that you will immediately use. Additional components can always be installed as needed
- **Turn off** unneeded services by setting the service to either Manual startup or Disabled
- Anti-Virus software installed on the server should be properly configured to exclude the file extensions used by SQL Server (mdf, ndf, ldf, bak, trn, log etc)

- Always stay as current version as possible.
- Pre-size your transaction log files and Data files and don't make them auto-grow.
- Separate transaction log files from data and tempdb volumes
- Size the tempdb database appropriately. For example, if you use the SORT_IN_TEMPDB option when you rebuild indexes, be sure to have sufficient free space in tempdb to store sorting operations.
- Use CHECKSUM on tempdb and User-defined databases
- Use Wait Stats and Windows System Monitor (perfmon) in conjunction to paint a picture of what is going on within the server.
- Use sys.dm_db_index_physical_stats to determine the extent of index fragmentation.
- Use the AUTO CREATE and AUTO UPDATE of statistics (the system default in SQL Server)
- Plan to use the backup compression feature of SQL Server 2008 Enterprise Edition.
- Backup LUN - Place backups on separate physical spindles. Do not back up to the same location as your database data files.
- Prefer sp_executesql than simply calling Exec @sql.
- Prefer "SELECT TOP (1)" to "SELECT TOP 1". The former is required by ANSI.
- The SQL Server services do not need to run under an administrator context or local system. It is recommended that you create a low privileged window account that you want the SQL Server service to run as
- Assume that damage is possible and have an aggressive backup policy. Back up all data regularly and store copies in a secure off-site location.
- Ensure that the mapping between database users and logins at the server level is correct. This can be a problem in cases where databases are detached and attached to other servers.
- Use Scope_Identity() rather than @@Identity.

For free SQL Server Performance Tuning Tips and Tricks subscribe here: https://go.sqlauthority.com

---

Consulting

Is your SQL Server running slow and you want to speed it up without sharing server credentials? In my **Comprehensive Database Performance Health Check**, we can work together remotely and resolve your biggest performance troublemakers in **less than 4 hours**.

Once you learn my business secrets, you will fix the majority of problems in the future.

Training

Have you ever opened any PowerPoint deck when you face SQL Server Performance Tuning emergencies? **SQL Server Performance Tuning Practical Workshop** is my MOST popular training with no PowerPoint presentations and **100% practical demonstrations**.

Essentially I share my business secrets to optimize SQL Server performance.

For **SQL Server Emergency Help**, you can reach out to me at *pinal@sqlauthority.com* with words ***URGENT*** in the email subject line for other services mention "*Comprehensive Database Performance Health Check*".

---

301 SQL Server Interview Questions and Answers Read for FREE here: https://blog.sqlauthority.com/category/sql-interview-questions-and-answers/

www.ingramcontent.com/pod-product-compliance
Ingram Content Group UK Ltd.
Pitfield, Milton Keynes, MK11 3LW, UK
UKHW022011190726
13853UKWH00004B/1880

9 798715 056337